WE SING WE STAY TOGETHER
SHABBAT MORNING SERVICE PRAYERS

HASHEM LIKES TO HEAR US
SINGING HIS PRAYERS.

King David, with his famous harp, near the entrance
to his tomb in Mount Zion, Jerusalem, Israel.

SING ALL THE WORDS FOR ALL THE PRAYERS
ARTSCROLL SIDDUR – ASHKENAZ

RICHARD COLLIS

wesingwestaytogether.com

The **We Sing We Stay Together**™ book of Shabbat Morning Service Prayers is designed to be used in conjunction with your regular siddur. The word "Siddur" literally means "order", and that is what it is; a book containing the prayers "in order".

First published in Great Britain 2019 by Richard Collis. Copyright © Richard Collis, 2019.

All rights reserved. No part of this publication may be reprinted or reproduced, stored in a retrieval system, or transmitted, in any form or by any means (electronic, mechanical, photocopying, recording, scanning or otherwise) without the prior written permission of the publisher.

This prayer book is sold subject to the condition that it shall not, by way of trade or otherwise, be lent, resold, hired out, or otherwise circulated without the prior written permission of the publisher, in any form of binding or cover other than that in which it is published and without a similar condition, including this condition, being imposed on the subsequent purchaser.

Richard Collis has asserted his moral and legal rights to be identified as the Compiler, Translator and Author of this work in accordance with the Copyright, Designs and Patents Act 1988.

Library of Congress Control Number: 2019913848

The "We Sing We Stay Together™" prayer book is available in six English language formats:

ISBN: 9781916111417 Paperback
ISBN: 9781916111424 Hardback
ISBN: 9781916111400 e-Book (Fixed interlinear layout)
ISBN: 9781916111431 e-Book (Dynamic reflowable layout)

For other languages, please refer to www.wesingwestaytogether.com

Artscroll / Mesorah Publications Ltd (www.artscroll.com) are the copyright holders of the Artscroll® Mesorah Series and have kindly given permission for their publications to be named as the reference sources for the authentic Hebrew prayer texts.

The trademark; We Sing We Stay Together™, is the property of Richard Collis and may not be used without prior written permission of the publisher.

Limit of liability/disclaimer of warranty: While the publisher and author, Richard Collis, has used his best efforts in preparing this prayer book, he makes no representations or warranties with respect to the accuracy or completeness of the contents of this prayer book and specifically disclaims any implied warranties of merchantability or fitness for a particular purpose. No warranty may be created or extended by sales representatives or written sales materials. The advice and strategies contained herein may not be suitable for your situation. You should consult with a professional where appropriate. No responsibility or liability for loss caused to any individual or organisation acting on, or refraining from action, as a result of the material in this publication can be accepted by the publisher and author, Richard Collis.

Every effort has been made to obtain the necessary permissions with reference to copyright material, both illustrative and written. Richard Collis apologizes for any omissions in this respect and will be pleased to make the appropriate acknowledgements in any future edition(s).

For the store, permissions, additional information and contact details, please visit www.wesingwestaytogether.com

Print and e-Book Distributor: Ingram Publisher Services, www.ingramspark.com
e-Book (English only) Distributor: Bookbaby, www.bookbaby.com

Shemot (Exodus) – Chapter 20, Verse 11.

For in six days Hashem made the heaven(s), and the earth, the sea and everything that is in them, and He rested on the seventh day – therefore, Hashem, blessed the Shabbat day and made it holy.

Beh-ezrat Hashem (with the help of Hashem) ב"ה

Preface

Our Jewish prayers are beautiful love songs;
full of goodness, affection, adoration, hope, kindness and generosity.
They are our DNA, even if we do not know them, because these
prayers, our religion, have moulded the Jewish people;
our way of thinking, education, who we are, and what we represent.
Judaism is all about being good and positive for oneself, family,
community, the wider world – all out of respect and love for Hashem*.
It fills me with gratitude, humility, and pride.

Community is all about family and friends, and we are all
friends, it is actually written in one of our prayers[1].
Friends sing together, it so warms our hearts.

Singing a prayer is not like singing a song, they are not just any words.
Some are crying out to be sung with great happiness[2]
because we love Hashem with all our heart, and all our soul[3].
Some tell us to sanctify clearly and harmoniously[4], and that
Hashem wants us to sing tuneful songs of praise to Him[5].
Some are serious, some sad, some educational, but all were written
with intent and purpose by the greatest scholars ever produced
by our people.

When we share prayer melodies we are connected and
together forever, and when we sing together we stay together
because there is that lovely feeling of being amongst friends.

AM ISRAEL CHAI – the people of Israel live.
With love, and hope for our children,

Richard Collis

Literally, * Hashem means "the Name" referring to God, and Shabbat means "rest".

1. Mi Sh'asa (track 36)
2. Ezrat avotanu (track 16)
3. Shma Israel, paragraph 1 (track 11)
4. Et shem ha'El (track 08)
5. Shochen ad (track 02)

There are so many other prayers which also encourage us to sing; check out the Anim zmirot (track 63) "Please place my abundance of songs before You, and my joyous singing will come close to You".

Shabbat Shachrit (Part 1 of 2)

Pg.	Trk	Artscroll page Interlinear**	Expanded*	Title
06	01	307–311	400–402	Nishmat col chai
08	02	312–314	404	Shochen ad
09	03	315–316	406	Yitgadal, No 1 Half Kaddish
09	04	317	406	Barchoo
10	05	318–320	408	Ha'col yoducha
11	06	321–323	410	El Adon
12	07	323–325	410–412	La'El asher shavat
13	08	326–327	412	Et shem ha'El
14	09	327–328	412	L'El baruch
15	10	328–330	412–414	Ahava raba
16	11	330–331	414	Shema Prayer; Shma Israel, paragraph 1
17	12	331–333	414–416	Shema Prayer; Ve'haya im shamoa, paragraph 2
18	13	333–334	416	Shema Prayer; Va'yomer Adonai, paragraph 3
19	14	334–335	416	Ve'yatziv
19	15	336	418	Al ha'rishonim
20	16	336–339	418–420	Ezrat avotanu
21	17	339–341	420	Amidah 1: Baruch ata Adonai
22	18	341	420	Amidah 1: Mechalkel chaim
23	19	342–343	422	Amidah 1: Nekadesh
24	20	344–346	424	Amidah 1: Yismach moshe, Ve'shamru & Ve'lo netato
25	21	346–347	424	Amidah 1: Elohanu
25	22	347–348	426	Amidah 1: Retze & Ve'techezeyna
26	23	348–351	426–428	Amidah 1: Modim
27	24	352–353	428–430	Amidah 1: Elohanu v'Elohai avotanu barchanu & Sim shalom
28	25	355–357	430–432	Yitgadal, No 1 Full Kaddish
29	26	357–358	432	Ain kamocha
30	27	358–359	432	Vayehi binsoah
31	28	362–364	436	Brich shmai
32	29	364–367	436–438	Shma Israel, Gadlu, Al ha'col & Av ha'rachamim
35	30	376	444	Yitgadal, No 2 Half Kaddish
36	31	377	444	V'zot ha'Torah
36	32	377–378	444	Etz chaim he
38	33	383–385	448–450	Yekum pourkan
39	34	385–386	450	Mi sh'berach

Blessings of New Month (only once per month)

Pg.	Trk	Interlinear	Expanded	Title
40	35	387–388	452	Yehi ratzon
41	36	388	452	Mi sh'asa
41	37	389	452	Rosh chodesh
41	38	389	452	Yechadshayhoo
42	39	391–393	454–456	Memorial Prayer; Av ha'rachamim shochen
44	40	393–395	456–458	Ashrei yoshvei
45	41	396	458	Y'halleloo et shem
46	42	397–399	458	Mizmor leDavid
47	43	399–400	460	Oovenucho yomar
48	44	400–401	460	Yitgadal, No 3 Half Kaddish

Shabbat Mussaf (Part 2 of 2)

Pg.	Trk	Artscroll page Interlinear**	Expanded*	Title
50	45	402–403	462	Amidah 2: Baruch ata Adonai
51	46	403	462	Amidah 2: Mechalkel chaim
52	47	404–405	464	Amidah 2: Naaritzcha
53	48	406–409	466	Amidah 2: Tikanta Shabbat
54	49	410–412	468	Amidah 2: Ooveyom ha'Shabbat & Yismechu
55	50	412–413	468	Amidah 2: Elohanu
56	51	414	470	Amidah 2: Retze & Ve'techezeyna
57	52	414–417	470–472	Amidah 2: Modim
58	53	417–418	472	Amidah 2: Elohanu v'Elohai avotanu barchanu & Sim shalom
59	54	420–422	474	Yitgadal, No 2, Full Kaddish
60	55	422	476	Kaveh
60	56	422–423	476	Ain ke'Elohanu
61	57	423–424	476	P'toum ha'ketoret
61	58	424–425	476–478	Raban Shimon
62	59	425–426	478	Ha'shir sh'haLeviyim
63	60	426–428	478	Tana d'vai Eliyahu & Amar Rabbi Elazar
64	61	430–432	480–482	Aleynu Leshabayach & Al ken nekave
65	62	432	482	Al tira
66	63	434–438	484–486	Anim zmirot
68	64	129	12	Adon olam

* Artscroll, The Expanded Siddur (Wasserman Edition).
** Artscroll, Sabbath & Festivals, Interlinear Siddur (Shottenstein Edition).

Shabbat Shachrit (of the Dawn)
The first section of the Morning Service
Part 1 of 2

Track 01 **Nishmat col chai** The soul of every living being

Artscroll, Expanded: Pages 400–402, Interlinear pages 307–311.

WE RECOGNISE THAT IT IS BEYOND OUR ABILITIES TO THANK HASHEM ENOUGH FOR ALL HIS BLESSINGS AND LOVE. A REMINDER TO BE HUMBLE AND APPRECIATE ALL THE GOOD THINGS WE HAVE IN LIFE.

Ni-shmat col chai, teva-rech et shim-cha, Adonai Eloheynou, veh-rou-ach col ba-sar
The soul (inside) of every living being will bless Your Name, Hashem, our God, and the spirit of all flesh

teh-fa-er oute-romem zich-reh-cha Mal-keh-nou ta-miyd.
will always glorify and exalt Your remembrance, our King.

Min ha-oh-lam veh-ad ha-oh-lam ah-ta El.
From the (start) of the world and to the (future) world, You are God.

Ou-mi-bala-deyh-cha ain la-nou Meh-lech goh-el ou-moh-shiya, po-deh ou-matziyl
And other than You, we have no King, Redeemer and Savior, who liberates, and rescues,

ou-meh-farnes ou-meh-ra-chem beh-chol et tzara veh-tzouka.
and provides, and is merciful at every time of trouble and woe.

Ain la-nou Meh-lech eh-la ah-ta.
We have no King but You.

Elohey ha-rish-oniym veha-ah-cha-roniym, Eloha col bri-yot, Ah-don col toladot,
God of the first (generations) and (through to) the last (generations), God of all creatures, Master of all generations,

ha-meh-houlal beh-rov ha-tish-ba-chot, ha-meh-na-heg oh-lamo beh-cheh-sed ou-vriy-otav
who is extolled through so many praises, who guides His world with loving kindness and His creatures

beh-rach-amiym. Va-Adonai lo ya-noum veh-lo yi-shan ha-meh-orer yeh-sh-niym
with mercy. And Hashem neither slumbers nor sleeps, He wakes the sleeping

veh-ha-meh-kiytz nir-da-miym, veh-ha-meh-siy-ach il-miym, veh-ha-ma-tiyr ah-sou-riym,
and stirs those who slumber, and He makes the mute speak, and He frees the captives,

veh-ha-soh-mech nof-liym, veh-ha-zo-kef kfou-fiym.
and He supports the fallen, and He straightens up the hunched.

Leh-cha leh-vad-cha ah-nach-nou moh-diym.
To You alone we give thanks.

Ilou piy-nou maleh shiyra ka-yam, oul-sho-nenou rina ka-hamon ga-lav,
Even if our mouth was as full of song as the sea (is with water), and our tongue as joyous (with song) as the roar of its waves,

veh-sifto-teynou sh-vach keh-mer-cha-vey ra-kiya, veh-eyney-nou meh-iy-rot
and our lips (as full) of praise as the expanses of the heavens (are broad), and our eyes as bright

ka-sh-mesh veh-cha-ya-reh-ach, veh-yadey-nou prou-sot keh-nishrey shamai-yim,
as the sun and the moon, and (even if) our hands are as spread out (as the wings) of eagles (of the) sky,

veh-ragley-nou ka-lot ka-ai-yalot, ain ah-nachnou maspi-kiym leh-hodot leh-cha, Adonai
and our feet as light (agile/swift) as (those of) deer, we would still not be capable of thanking You (enough), Hashem,

Eloheynou veh-Elohey avoteynou, ou-leh-va-rech et shmeh-cha al ah-chat meh-alef
our God, and the God of our forefathers, nor of blessing Your Name (enough), for (even) one from the thousand

eh-lef al-fey ala-fiym veh-ribey reh-va-vot peh-amiym ha-tovot sh-asiyta im avoteynou
of thousands, and many tens of thousands of good things that You have done for our forefathers,

veh-ima-nou. Mi mitzrai-yim geh-al-tanou Adonai Eloheynou, ou-mi-beyt ava-diym
and for us. From Egypt, You, Hashem, our God, redeemed us, and from the house of slaves

Shabbat Shachrit (Part 1)

pdiy-tanou, beh-ra-av zan-tanou, ou-veh-soh-va kil-kal-tanou, meh-cheh-rev hitz-al-tanou,
You freed us, in famine You fed us, and in (with) plenty You sustained us, from the sword You saved us,

ou-mi-deh-ver mila-teh-tanou, ou-meh-choh-lai-yim ra-iym veh-neh-eh-ma-niym,
and from plague You rescued us, and from nasty and steadfast illnesses

di-liy-ta-anou.
You spared us.

Ad heh-na aza-rou-nou racha-meyh-cha, veh-lo aza-vou-nou cha-sa-deyh-cha.
Until now Your mercy has helped us, and Your loving kindness has never left us.

Veh-al tit-sh-eh-nou Adonai Eloheynou la-netz-ach. Ahl ken eh-va-riym sh-pi-lagta
And (please) do not abandon us, Hashem, our God, never ever. For (all) this, the organs that You arranged

ba-nou, veh-rou-ach ou-neh-shama sh-na-fach-ta beh-ah-peynou, veh-la-shon ah-sher
within us, and the spirit and soul that You blew into our noses, and the tongue that

samm-ta beh-fiy-nou, hen hem yodou vi-yev-ar-chou vi-yesh-ab-chou vi-yifa-ah-rou
You placed in our mouth, they themselves will (all) thank, and bless, and praise, and glorify,

vi-yi-romemou veh-ya-aritz-ou veh-yakdi-iyshou veh-yamli-iy-chou et shim-cha mal-kenou.
and exalt, and venerate, and sanctify, and declare Your Name as sovereign, our King.

Ki col peh leh-cha yo-deh, veh-chol la-shon leh-cha tish-ava, veh-chol beh-rech
For every mouth will thank You, and every tongue will swear (allegiance) to You, and every knee

leh-cha tich-ra, veh-chol koma leh-fa-neyh-cha tishta-cha-veh, veh-chol leh-vavot
will bend to You, and every spine will bow to You, and all hearts

yira-ou-cha, veh-chol keh-rev ouch-lai-yot yez-amrou lish-meh-cha, ka-davar
will fear You, and all innermost emotions (in all people) will sing praises to Your Name, as the declaration (word)

sh-ka-touv: col atz-motai toh-marna, Adonai mi ka-moh-cha, ma-tziyl ani meh-chazak
was written: All my bones will say, Hashem, who is like You, who saves the poor (man) from the (man) who is stronger
PSALM 35:10

mi-menou, veh-ani veh-ev-yon mi-gozlo. Mi yidmeh lach, oumi yishveh lach,
than him, and (saves) the poor and wretched (man) from his robber? Who is similar to You, and who is equal to You,

oumi ya-a-rach lach. Ha-El ha-ga-dol ha-gibor veh-ha-norah, El el-yon,
and who can be compared to You? The God who is Great, Mighty, and Awesome, the supreme God,

koh-neh shmai-yim va-aretz. Neh-ha-lel-cha ou-nesha-beh-cheh-cha ou-neh-fa-er-cha
creator of heaven and earth. We will praise You, and will laud You, and will glorify You,

ou-neh-va-rech et shem kod-sh-cha, ka-amour leh-David, bar-chi nafshi et Adonai,
and will bless Your holy Name, as was said, by (King) David, O my soul bless Hashem,

veh-chol kra-vai et shem kodsho.
PSALM 103:1
and may all that is within me (bless) His holy Name.

Ha-El beh-ta-atzou-mot ouz-eh-cha, ha-gadol bich-vod shmeh-cha, ha-gibor
The God, in the absoluteness of Your might, the Great One, in (the) glory of Your Name, the Mighty One

la-netz-ach veh-ha-nora beh-nohr-oh-teyh-cha.
forever, and the Amazing One in Your awesomeness.

Ha-Meh-lech ha-yo-shev al ki-seh ram veh-nisa.
The King who sits on the high and exalted throne.

Track 02 **Shochen ad** He abides forever

Artscroll, Expanded: Page 404, Interlinear pages 312–314

**THE PRAYER LEADER IS CALLING US TOGETHER TO SING FROM OUR HEARTS
THE MOST BEAUTIFUL AND TUNEFUL SONGS OF PRAISE TO HASHEM.**

Shoh-chen ad marom veh-ka-dosh shmo. Veh-ka-touv:
He abides forever, exalted and holy is His Name. And it is written:

PSALM 33:1
ra-nenou tzadi-kiym ba-Adonai lai-sha-riym na-ava teh-hila.
sing joyfully, (you) righteous ones for Hashem, (because) for the upright (honest) it is befitting to praise (Him).

Beh-fi yesh-ah-riym tit-ha-lal, ouv-divrey tzadi-kiym tit-ba-rach,
By (in) the mouth of the upright (honest) You will be praised, and through (in) the words of the righteous You will be blessed,

ou-vil-shon chasi-diym tit-ro-ma-am ou-veh-keh-rev kdosh-iym titka-da-ash.
and by (in) the tongue of the devout You will be exalted, and amongst holy people You will be sanctified.

Ou-veh-mak-helot riveh-vot am-cha beyt Israel, beh-rina
And in the tens of thousands of congregations of Your people, the House of Israel, in joyful song,

yitpa-ar shim-cha Malkeh-nou, beh-chol dor va-dor, sh-ken cho-vat col heitz-ou-riym,
Your Name will be glorified, our King, in every generation, for it is the duty of all (Your) creations,

leh-fa-neyh-cha Adonai Eloheynou veh-Elohey avoteynou, leh-hodot leh-ha-lel
in Your presence (before You), Hashem, our God, and God of our forefathers, to thank, to laud,

leh-sha-beh-ach leh-fa-er leh-romem leh-ha-der leh-va-rech leh-a-leh ou-leh-ka-less,
to praise, to glorify, to exalt, to honor, to bless, to extol, and to sing praises (to You),

al col divrey shiy-rot veh-tish-beh-chot David ben Yishai
better than all the words, songs and praises of (King) David, son of Jesse,

av-deh-cha meshiy-cheh-cha.
Your servant (and) Your anointed one.

Yishta-bach shim-cha la-ad mal-kenou, ha-El ha-Meh-lech ha-gadol veh-ha-kadosh,
Your Name, our King, will be praised forever, the God, the King, the Great One and the Holy One,

ba-sha-mai-yim ou-va-aretz. Ki leh-cha na-eh, Adonai Eloheynou veh-Elohey
in heaven and on earth. For it is pleasant for You, Hashem, our God, and God

avoteynou*, shiyr ou-shva-cha halel veh-zimra, oz ou-mem-shala netzach gdoula
of our forefathers, (that there be) song, and praise, adulation, and hymns, strength, and dominion, victory, greatness,

ou-gvoura teh-hila veh-tif-eh-ret kdou-sha ou-mal-choute, bra-chot veh-ho-da-ot
and might, laudation, and splendor, holiness, and sovereignty, blessings, and gratitudes,

meh-ata veh-ad oh-lam. Barouch ata Adonai El Meh-lech gadol batish-ba-chot,
from now and onwards forever. Blessed are You, Hashem, God, King, (Whose) greatness (is celebrated) in praises,

El ha-hoda-ot Ah-don ha-nif-la-ot, ha-boch-er beh-shiy-rey zimra,
God (to Whom we give) thanks, Master of wonders, who chooses tuneful songs of praise,

Meh-lech El chey ha-oh-la-miym.
King, God, who (gives) life to the worlds.

* *The word "Avoteynou" appears many times in our prayers. Literally it means "Our Fathers",
but actually refers to our forefathers, the Patriarchs: Abraham, Isaac and Jacob.*

Shabbat Shachrit (Part 1)

Track 03 **Yitgadal, No 1 Half Kaddish**

Artscroll, Expanded: Page 406, Interlinear pages 315–316.

FIRST OF 3 IN SHABBAT MORNING SERVICE.

HASHEM CREATED THE WORLD AS HE WANTED IT.
WE HAVE TO MEET THE CHALLENGES OF THIS WORLD.

Yitgadal veh-yit-kadash shmeh raba. Beh-olma di bra kir-ou-teh
May His great Name be magnified and sanctified. In the world that He created as He wanted it,

veh-yamliych malchou-teh, beh-chai-yey-chon ou-veh-yo-mey-chon ouv-chai-yey
may His Kingship reign, in your lifetimes, and in your days, and in the lifetimes

deh-chol bet Israel, ba-agala ouvi-zman ka-riyv. Veh-imrou amen.
of all of the House of Israel, speedily and soon. And we say: Amen.

Yeh-heh shmeh raba meh-vo-rach leh-oh-lam ou-leh-olmey olmai-ya.
May His great Name be blessed forever, and for all eternity.

Yit-barach veh-yishtabach veh-yitpa-ar veh-yitromam veh-yitna-seh veh-yit-hadar
Blessed, and praised, and glorified, and exalted, and upraised, and honored,

veh-yit-ah-leh veh-yit-ha-lal shmeh deh-koud-sha briych hou.
and elevated, and extolled, is the Name of the Holy One, Blessed is He.

Leh-elah min col bir-cha-ta veh-shiy-rata, toush-beh-cha-ta veh-neh-cheh-mata
Way above any blessing, and song, praise, and cheer

da-amiyran beh-olma. Veh-imrou amen.
that are vocalized in the world. And we say: Amen

Track 04 **Barchoo** Let us bless

Artscroll, Expanded: Page 406, Interlinear page 317.

THIS IS THE START OF THE PRAYERS LEADING TO THE SHEMA PRAYER.

Bar-chou et Adonai hamm-vo-rach.
Bless Hashem, the Blessed One.

Barouch Adonai hamm-vo-rach leh-oh-lam va-ed.
Blessed is Hashem, the Blessed One, forever and ever.

Barouch ata Adonai Eloheynou Meh-lech ha-oh-lam, yo-tzer orr ou-vo-reh chosh-ech,
Blessed are You Hashem, our God, King of the world, who makes light and creates darkness,

oh-seh shalom ou-vo-reh et ha-col.
who makes peace and creates everything.

Shabbat Shachrit (Part 1)

Track 05 **Ha'col yoducha** All will thank You

Artscroll, Expanded: Page 408, Interlinear pages 318–320.

WE THANK HASHEM FOR BRINGING LIGHT TO THE WORLD AND PROVIDING US WITH STRENGTH.

Ha-col yoh-dou-cha veh-ha-col yeh-shab-chou-cha veh-ha-col yom-rou ain kadosh
All will thank You, and all will praise You, and all will say that nothing is holy

ka-Adonai. Ha-col yeh-roh-meh-mou-cha selah, yoh-oh-tzer ha-col.
like Hashem. All will exalt You forever, (You) Creator of everything.

Ha-El ha-poh-teh-ach beh-chol yom dal-tot sha-a-rey miz-rach ou-voh-keh-a
The God who every day opens the doors of the gateways of (facing) the east, and splits open

cha-loh-ney ra-kiy-a, mo-tziy cha-ma mim-koma oul-vana mim-chon shivta,
the windows of the heavens, pulls out the sun (the hot one) from its place, and the moon (the white one) from its dwelling spot,

ou-meh-iyr la-oh-lam koulo oul-yosh-vav, sh-bara beh-midat rach-amiym.
and (so) lights up the whole world, and its dwellers, that He created in (His) merciful way.

Ha-meh-iyr la-aretz veh-la-da-riym ah-lay-ha beh-rach-amiym, ouv-tou-vo
He lights up the earth, and its inhabitants with mercy, and in His goodness

meh-cha-desh beh-chol yom ta-miyd ma-aseh beh-reh-shiyt.
renews, every day, perpetually (day after day), His act of creation.

Ha-Meh-lech hamm-romam leh-vado meh-az,
The King, who alone was exalted from way back (the beginning),

hamm-shou-bach veh-ha-meh-fo-ar veh-hamit-na-seh miy-mot oh-lam.
who was praised, and glorified and upraised, from the days of (the creation of) the world.

Elohey oh-lam beh-racham-eyh-cha ha-ra-biym ra-chem ah-ley-nou,
God of the world with Your abundant mercy, have mercy on us,

Ah-don ou-zenou, tzour misga-benou, magen yish-enou, misgav ba-ad-enou.
Master of our strength, Rock of our stronghold, Shield of our salvation, (You are) a stronghold (shelter) for us.

Ain keh-er-keh-cha, veh-ain zou-la-teh-cha,
Nothing compares to You, and (there is) nothing other than You,

eh-fes bil-teh-cha, ou-mi doh-meh lach. Ain keh-er-keh-cha Adonai Eloheynou
(there is) zero without You, and who is similar to You? Nothing compares to You, Hashem, our God,

ba-oh-lam ha-zeh, veh-ain zou-lat-cha Mal-keh-nou leh-cha-yey ha-oh-lam ha-ba.
in this world, and (there is) nothing except for You, our King, in the life of the world to come.

Eh-fes bil-teh-cha goh-ah-lenou liy-mot ha-mashiy-ach, veh-ain doh-meh leh-cha
(There) is zero without You, our Redeemer in the days of the Messiah, and (there is) nothing similar to You,

moshi-enou lit-chi-yat ha-met-iym.
our Savior, (at the time when) the dead are brought back to life (by You).

Shabbat Shachrit (Part 1)

Track 06 **El Adon** God, the Master

Artscroll, Expanded: Page 410, Interlinear pages 321–323.

HASHEM CREATED THE GREAT LIGHTS, THE SUN AND MOON, THAT ILLUMINATE THE WORLD.

El Ah-don al col hama-a-siym, barouch ou-meh-vo-rach beh-fi col nesh-ama,
God, the Master of all deeds (actions), the Blessed One, and who is blessed by the mouth of every soul,

godd-lo veh-touvo ma-leh oh-lam, da-at ou-tvouna soh-veh-viym oto. Ha-mit-ga-eh
His greatness and His goodness fill the world, knowledge and insight surround Him. The Exalted One

al cha-yot ha-ko-desh, veh-neh-hedar beh-cha-vod al ha-mer-kava, zchoute
above the holy Chayot angels, and fantastic in (His) glory above the (Celestial) Chariot, merit

ou-miy-shor lif-ney kis-oh, cheh-sed veh-racha-miym lif-ney kvodo.
and fairness emanate from (are before) His throne, loving kindness and mercies emanate from (are before) His glory.

Tov-iym meh-orot sh-bara Eloheynou, yeh-tza-ram beh-da-at beh-viy-na
Good are the (great) lights that our God has created, He made them with knowledge, understanding

ou-veh-hass-kel, ko-ach ou-gvoura natan ba-hem, lihi-yot mosh-liym
and intelligence, He gave them strength and might, (so that) they would be dominant

beh-keh-rev teh-vel.
within the world.

Mleh-iym ziyv ou-meh-fi-kiym noga, na-eh ziy-vam beh-chol ha-oh-lam,
Full of gloss and radiating brightness, their glow is beautiful throughout the world,

smech-iym beh-tzeh-tam veh-sa-siym beh-vo-am, oh-siym beh-ey-mah reh-tzon
they are happy when they set off, and they rejoice when they return, in awe they do the will of

koh-nam.
their Creator.

Peh-er veh-cha-vod not-niym lish-mo, tza-hala veh-rina leh-zeh-cher
They give splendor and honor to His Name, (and they give) joy and song to remember

mal-chouto, ka-ra la-sh-mesh va-yiz-rach orr,
His Kingdom, He called out to the sun and it shone (its) light,

ra-a veh-hit-kiyn tzou-rat ha-leh-vana.
He saw and arranged the form (phases) of the moon (the white one).

Sh-vach not-niym lo col tzva ma-arom.
All the (angelic) host up on high give Him praise.

Tif-eh-ret ou-gdoula, sra-fiym veh-ofa-niym veh-cha-yot ha-ko-desh.
Splendor and greatness (are bestowed on Him by) the Seraphim, and Ophanim and the holy Chayot angels.

Shabbat Shachrit (Part 1)

Track 07 **La'El asher shavat** To the God who rested

Artscroll, Expanded: Pages 410–412, Interlinear pages 323–325.

**HASHEM DESERVEDLY RESTED AFTER HIS GREAT WORKS OF CREATING THE WORLD AND WANTED TO GIFT US THE SAME DELIGHT;
THE HOLY SHABBAT DAY OF TOTAL BLISS AND REST.**

La-El ah-sher sha-vat mi-col ha-ma-a-siym, ba-yom ha-shvi-iy hit-ala veh-ya-shav al
To the God who rested from all His works; on the seventh day (Shabbat) He ascended and sat on

kiseh kvodo, tif-eh-ret ata leh-yom ha-meh-nou-cha, oneg kara leh-yom ha-Shabbat,
the throne of His glory, He wrapped the day of rest in splendor, (and) called the Shabbat Day a delight,

zeh sh-vach shel yom ha-shvi-iy, sh-bo sha-vat El mi-col meh-lach-toh.
(so) this is the praise of the seventh day, on which God rested from all His work.

Veh-yom ha-shvi-iy meh-sha-beh-ach veh-omer: Mizmor shiyr leh-yom ha-shabbat,
And the seventh day (itself) praises and vocalizes: A psalm, a song for the (honor of the) Shabbat Day,

PSALM 92:1–2

tov leh-hodot la-Adonai.
it is good to thank Hashem.

Leh-fiy-chach yeh-fa-a-rou vi-yeh-var-chou la-El col yeh-tzou-rav.
Therefore, all (those) He created will glorify and bless God.

Sh-vach yeh-kar oug-dou-lah yitnou leh-El Meh-lech yotzer col, ha-mann-chiyl
Praise, honor, and greatness they will give to the God, the King who makes everything, who bequeathed

meh-nou-cha leh-amo Israel bik-dou-sha-toh beh-yom Shabbat ko-desh.
respite to His people Israel, in His holiness, on the holy Shabbat day.

Shim-cha Adonai Eloheynou yitka-dash, veh-zich-reh-cha Mal-kenou yitpa-ar,
Your Name Hashem, our God, will be sanctified, and remembrance of You, our King, will be glorified,

ba-shamai-yim mi-ma-al veh-al ha-aretz mi-tach-at. Titba-rach mo-shiy-enou
in the heavens above and on the earth below. You will be blessed, our Savior,

al sh-vach ma-aseh ya-deyh-cha, veh-al meh-orey orr sh-asiyta yeh-fa-arou-cha selah.
for (all) the praiseworthy works of Your hands; and for (all) the (great) lights that You made, You will be glorified forever.

Tit-ba-rach tzour-eh-nou Malkeh-eh-nou veh-goh-ah-leh-nou, boreh kedosh-iym.
You will be blessed, our Rock, our King, and our Redeemer, Creator of holy ones.

Yishta-bach shim-cha la-ad Malkeh-nou, yo-tzer meh-shar-tiym, va-ah-sher
Your Name, our King, will be praised forever, Creator of ministering angels, and whose

meh-shar-tav koulam om-diym beh-roum oh-lam, ou-mashmiy-iym beh-yir-a
ministering angels all stand at the summit of the world, and they make heard in awe (fear),

ya-chad beh-kol divrey Elohim chai-yim ou-Meh-lech oh-lam. Koulam ah-hou-viym,
in unison, out loud, the words of the living God, and King of the world. They are all beloved,

koulam brou-riym, koulam gibo-riym, veh-chou-lam oh-siym beh-ey-ma ouv-yir-ah
they are all flawless, they are all mighty, and they all perform with trepidation and awe (fear),

reh-tzon koh-oh-nam. Veh-chou-lam pot-chiym et piy-hem bik-dou-sha
the will of their Maker. And they all open their mouths in holiness,

ou-veh-toh-hara, beh-shiyra ou-veh-zimra, ou-meh-var-chiym ou-meh-shab-chiym
and in purity, in song and in hymn, and they bless, and they praise,

ou-meh-fa-a-riym ou-ma-ar-iytz-iym ou-mak-diysh-iym ou-mamm-liy-chiym:
and they glorify, and they revere, and they sanctify and they declare the Kingship of – (leads onto track 08).

Shabbat Shachrit (Part 1)

Track 08 Et shem ha'El The Name of God

Artscroll, Expanded: Page 412, Interlinear pages 326–327.

THE ANGELS CALL ON EACH OTHER TO PRAISE HASHEM CLEARLY AND HARMONIOUSLY.

Et shem ha-El, ha-Meh-lech ha-gadol ha-gibor veh-ha-nora ka-dosh hou.
The Name of the God, the King, the Great One, the Mighty One and the Awesome One, He is Holy.

Veh-chou-lam meh-ka-bliym ah-ley-hem ol mal-choute shamai-yim zeh mi-zeh,
All (the angels) accept upon themselves, from each other, the yoke of the sovereignty of heaven,

veh-not-niym resh-oute zeh la-zeh (veh-not-niym resh-oute zeh la-zeh),
and (the angels) give permission to one another (and the angels give permission to one another),

leh-hak-diysh leh-yotz-ram beh-na-chat rou-ach beh-safa brou-ra ouvi-neh-iyma,
to sanctify their Maker, with calmness (contentment) of spirit, in clear and harmonious (pleasant) language,

kedou-sha kou-lam keh-eh-chad oh-niym veh-om-riym beh-yir-ah:
(with an affirmation of His) holiness, all of them as one, responding and proclaiming in awe (fear):

Kadosh kadosh kadosh Adonai tzva-ot mlo col ha-aretz kvoh-doh.
Holy, holy, holy is Hashem, (Lord) of the armies (of Israel), the whole earth (land) is filled with His glory.

Veh-ha-oh-fa-niym veh-cha-yot ha-ko-desh beh-ra-ash gadol mitnas-iym
And (then) the Ofanim (angels) and holy Chayot (angels), with great noise stand up

leh-ou-mat sra-fiym, leh-ou-ma-tam meh-shab-chiym veh-om-riym:
facing the Seraphim (angels), (once) facing them they praise and proclaim:

Barouch kvod Adonai mim-komo.
Blessed is the glory of Hashem from His place.

Shabbat Shachrit (Part 1)

Track 09 L'El baruch To the Blessed God

Artscroll, Expanded: Page 412, Interlinear pages 327–328.

**THE ANGELS CONTINUE TO BLESS HASHEM WITH PLEASANT MELODIES.
WE ASK HASHEM TO SHINE HIS GOODNESS ON ISRAEL.**

Leh-El ba-rouch neh-iy-mot yit-enou. Leh-Meh-lech El chai veh-kai-yam,
To the Blessed God, they (the angels) will give pleasant melodies. To the King, the living and enduring God,

zmirot yo-mer-ou veh-tish-ba-chot yashmiy-ou, ki hou leh-vado poh-el gvourot,
they will sing hymns, and they will make the praises heard, because He alone performs mighty deeds,

oh-seh cha-dash-ot, ba-al mil-cha-mot, zo-reh-a tzad-akot,
makes new things, (and) is the Master of wars, (and) sows righteousnesses,

matz-miy-ach yeh-shou-ot, bo-reh refou-ot, nora teh-hilot,
(and) makes salvations sprout, (and) creates cures, (and) is awesome beyond praises,

Ah-don hanif-la-ot, ha-meh-cha-desh beh-touvo
(and) is the Master of wonders, (and) who in His goodness renews,

beh-chol yom ta-miyd ma-a-seh beh-reh-shiyt.
every day, perpetually (day after day), the work of the Creation (of the World).

PSALM 136:7

Ka-ah-mour leh-oh-seh or-iym gdo-liym, ki leh-oh-lam chas-doh.
As it is said: To the Maker of the great lights, for (because) His loving kindness is forever.

Orr cha-dash al tZi-yon ta-iyr, veh-niz-keh kou-la-nou meh-heh-ra leh-oh-ro.
Shine a new light on Zion, and may we all quickly benefit (be rewarded) from His (Hashem's) light.

Barouch ata Adonai, yo-tzer ha-meh-oh-rot.
Blessed are You, Hashem, who makes the (great) lights (the sun and moon).

Shabbat Shachrit (Part 1)

Track 10 **Ahava raba** With so much love

Artscroll, Expanded: Pages 412–414, Interlinear pages 328–330.

**HASHEM LOVES US AND WANTS US CLOSE TO HIM.
WE ASK HASHEM TO ENLIGHTEN US, TO HELP US IMPROVE AS PEOPLE
AND TO LEAD US BACK TO ISRAEL.**

Ah-hava raba ah-hav-tanou Adonai Eloheynou, chem-la gdola viy-teh-ra
With so much love You loved us, Hashem, our God, (with) great and excessive compassion,

cha-mal-ta ah-ley-nou.
You were merciful to us.

Aviy-nou mal-kenou, ba-a-vour avo-teynou sh-bat-chou beh-cha,
Our Father, our King, for the sake of our forefathers who trusted in You,

va-tel-am-dem chouk-ey chai-yim, ken teh-choh-ney-nou oute-lam-deh-nou.
and to whom You taught the laws of life, so (please) be gracious to us and teach us.

Aviy-nou ha-av ha-rach-aman ha-meh-ra-chem, rah-chem ah-leynou, veh-ten
Our Father, the Merciful Father, the Merciful One have mercy on us, and (please) give

beh-li-beh-nou leh-ha-viyn ou-leh-hass-kiyl, lishmo-a lil-mod ou-leh-la-med,
to our hearts (the ability) to understand and be enlightened, to listen, to learn, and to teach,

lishmor veh-la-asot ou-leh-ka-yem et col divrey tal-moud Torah-teh-cha beh-ah-hava.
to observe, and to perform, and to fulfill (realize) all the words (from the) study of Your Torah, with love.

Veh-ha-er ey-ney-nou beh-Torah-teh-cha, veh-da-bek lib-eh-nou
And light up our eyes in Your Torah, and glue our heart(s)

beh-mitzvo-teyh-cha, veh-ya-ched leh-va-venou leh-ah-hava oul-yir-a
to Your commandments, and dedicate our heart(s) to love and to fear (be in awe of)

et shmeh-cha, veh-lo neh-vosh leh-oh-lam va-ed ki beh-shem kod-sheh-cha
Your Name, and (because of this) we will never be ashamed again (of our behavior), because in Your holy Name,

ha-gadol veh-ha-nora ba-tach-nou, na-giyla veh-nis-meh-cha bi-yeshoua-teh-cha.
that is great and awesome, we have trust, (and) we will rejoice and we will be happy in Your salvation.

Va-ha-viy-enou leh-shalom meh-arba kan-fot ha-aretz, veh-toh-liych-enou
And (please) bring us in peace from the four corners of the earth, and lead us (back)

kommemi-youte leh-artz-enou. Ki El poh-el yeh-shou-ot ata, ou-vanou ba-charta
upright (with our heads held up high) to our land (Israel). For You are the God who performs salvations, and You chose us

mi-col am veh-la-shon. Veh-keh-rav-tanou leh-shim-cha ha-gadol selah
from (amongst) all peoples and tongues. And You brought us close to Your great Name, forever,

beh-eh-met, leh-ho-dot leh-cha ou-leh-ya-ched-cha beh-ah-hava.
(and) in truth, (for us) to thank You and to (proclaim) Your Oneness with love.

Barouch ata Adonai, ha-bo-cher beh-amo Israel beh-ah-hava.
Blessed are You, Hashem, who chooses in His people Israel, with love.

Shabbat Shachrit (Part 1)

Track 11 **Shema Prayer; Shma Israel, paragraph 1**

Artscroll, Expanded: Page 414, Interlinear pages 330–331.

THE SHEMA PRAYER
SHMA ISRAEL, HEAR O ISRAEL

These words beat in our hearts.

A declaration of our love of Hashem and gratitude that we are the Children of Israel.

These eternal words unite us for good every day
and connect us forever to all who came before.

Every time you say

SHMA ISRAEL

you are part of the story and continuation of Israel, the Jewish Nation.

SHMA ISRAEL, ADONAI ELOHEYNOU, ADONAI EH-CHAD.
Hear O Israel, Hashem is our God, Hashem is One.

(Barouch shem kvod malchou-toh leh-olam va-ed). *Said quietly to oneself.*
(Blessed is the name of His glorious Kingdom, forever and ever).

Veh-ah-havta et Adonai Elo-heyh-cha, beh-chol leh-vav-cha ou-veh-chol
And you will love Hashem, your God, with all your heart, and with all

naf-sheh-cha, ou-veh-chol meh-od-eh-cha:
your soul, and with all your all (everything you have):

Veh-ha-you ha-dva-riym ha-eh-leh, ah-sher ah-nochi metzav-cha ha-yom,
And these are the words (orders), that I command you today,

al leh-va-veh-cha: veh-shi-nan-tam leh-va-neyh-cha, veh-di-bar-ta bam
onto your heart: And you will (repeatedly) teach them to your children, and you will speak of them

beh-shiv-teh-cha beh-veyt-eh-cha, ou-veh-lech-teh-cha ba-deh-rech,
when you are sitting in your home, and when you are out walking on the path,

ou-veh-shoch-beh-cha ou-veh-kou-meh-cha: ouk-shar-tam leh-ot
and when you are lying down (as you go to sleep), and when you are getting up (as you wake up): And you will tie them as a sign

al ya-deh-cha, veh-ha-you leh-tota-fot beyn ey-neyh-cha:
on your arm, and they will be Tefillin between your eyes:

Ouch-tav-tam al meh-zouzot beyt-eh-cha ouvi-sh-ah-reyh-cha.
And you will write them on the door posts (as Mezuzot) of your home, and on your gates.

IT IS A COMMANDMENT FROM OUR TORAH TO RECITE
THE THREE PARAGRAPHS OF THE SHEMA PRAYER TWICE A DAY.

Shabbat Shachrit (Part 1)

Track 12 **Shema Prayer; Ve'haya im shamoa, paragraph 2**

Artscroll, Expanded: Pages 414–416, Interlinear pages 331–333.

WE ALSO HAVE RESPONSIBILITIES TO MAINTAIN OUR RELATIONSHIP WITH HASHEM. HASHEM WANTS US TO APPRECIATE OUR GOOD FORTUNE AND REMEMBER THE IMPORTANCE OF HIS COMMANDMENTS.

Veh-ha-ya im shamo-a tish-meh-ou el mitzvo-tai
And it will be (happen), if you listen to and hear (take heed of) My commandments,

ah-sher ah-nochi metza-veh et-chem ha-yom,
that I command (instruct) you today,

leh-ah-hava et Adonai Elo-hey-chem ou-leh-ovdo beh-chol leh-vav-chem
to love Hashem, your God, and to serve Him with all your heart

ou-veh-chol naf-sheh-chem: Veh-na-ta-ti metar artz-eh-chem beh-ito yoreh
and with all your soul. I will give rain to your land at the right time, the first rain (of autumn)

ou-mal-kosh veh-ah-saf-ta dgan-eh-cha veh-tiy-rosh-cha veh-yitz-ha-reh-cha:
and the last rain (of spring), and you will harvest your grain, and your wine and your (olive) oil:

Veh-na-ta-ti eh-sev beh-sadd-cha liv-hem-teh-cha, veh-ah-chal-ta veh-sa-va-ta:
I will provide grass in your field(s) for your cattle, and you will eat and you will be satisfied:

Hish-amrou la-chem pen yif-teh leh-vav-chem, veh-sar-tem va-ava-deh-tem
Beware not to let your heart be seduced, and (cause you) to stray, and worship

Elohim ach-eh-riym veh-hish-ta-cha-viy-tem la-hem: Veh-chara aff Adonai ba-chem
other (false) deities, and bow down to them. And so ignite the anger of Hashem against you,

veh-atzar et ha-shamai-yim veh-lo yihi-yeh matar,
and (then) He will restrain the heaven(s), and there will be no rain,

veh-ha-adama lo ti-ten et yeh-voula,
and the land will not give its produce,

va-avadetem meh-heh-ra meh-al ha-aretz ha-tova ah-sher Adonai noten la-chem:
and you will quickly disappear (perish) from the good land that Hashem is giving you:

Veh-samm-tem et dva-rai eh-leh al leh-vav-chem veh-al naf-sh-chem,
And you will place these words of Mine on your heart, and on your soul,

ouk-shar-tem otam leh-ot al yed-chem, veh-ha-you leh-totafot beyn eyney-chem:
and you will tie them as a sign on your arm, and they will be Tefillin between your eyes:

Veh-lima-detem otam et beney-chem leh-da-ber bam,
And you will teach them to your children, (and you will) speak of them

beh-shiv-teh-cha beh-vey-teh-cha,
when you are sitting in your home,

ou-veh-lech-teh-cha ba-deh-rech, ou-veh-shoch-beh-cha ou-veh-kou-meh-cha:
and when you are out walking on the path, and when you are lying down (going to sleep), and when you are getting up (waking up):

Ouch-tav-tam al meh-zouzot beyt-eh-cha ouvi-sh-a-reyh-cha.
And you will write them on the door posts (as Mezuzot) of your home, and on your gates.

Leh-ma-an yirbou yeh-mey-chem vi-yi-mey bney-chem al ha-adama
So as to multiply your days, and the days of your children, on the land (of Israel)

Shabbat Shachrit (Part 1)

ah-sher nish-ba Adonai la-avo-tey-chem la-tet la-hem,
that Hashem promised to your forefathers, to give it to them,

ki-yimey ha-shamai-yim al ha-aretz.
for (all) the days (that) the heavens are above the earth.

Track 13 Shema Prayer; Va'yomer Adonai, paragraph 3

Artscroll, Expanded: Page 416, Interlinear pages 333–334.

**HASHEM EXPLAINED THE REASON FOR THE COMMANDMENT TO WEAR TZITZIT.
A VISUAL REMINDER FOR EVERYONE TO ALWAYS BE AWARE OF RIGHT AND WRONG.**

Va-yo-mer Adonai el Moshe leh-eh-mor:
And Hashem spoke to Moses saying:

Da-ber el bney Israel veh-amarta ah-ley-hem,
Speak to the Children of Israel and tell them (to do as follows);

veh-a-sou la-hem tziy-tzit al kan-fey big-dey-hem leh-doh-ro-tam,
and (so) they made for themselves Tzitzit on the corners of their clothes for (all) their generations,

veh-nat-nou al tziy-tzit ha-kanaf ptiyl tche-let:
and they put on (every) corner of the Tzitzit, a (tinted azure blue) thread of techeilet:

Veh-ha-ya la-chem leh-tziy-tzit, oor-iy-tem oto ou-zcharr-tem et col mitzvot Adonai
And it will be for you Tzitzit, and (each time) you will see them (the Tzitzit), you will remember all of the commandments of Hashem,

va-asiy-tem otam, veh-lo ta-tou-rou achrey leh-vav-chem veh-ach-rey ey-ney-chem
and you will perform them, and you will not seek after (any impure desires) of your heart, and nor after (any impure desires) of your eyes,

ah-sher atem zo-niym achrey-hem: Leh-ma-an tiz-kerou va-asiy-tem et col mitz-votai,
lest you debase (yourselves) after them. (And) so you will remember and perform all of My commandments,

vi-hyiy-tem kdosh-iym leh-Elohey-chem:
and you will be holy (people) to your God.

Ani Adonai Elo-hey-chem ah-sher hoh-tzeti et-chem meh-eretz mitzrai-yim
I am Hashem, your God, who brought you out from the land of Egypt,

lihi-yot la-chem leh-Elohim, ani Adonai Elohey-chem eh-met
to be for you a God, I am Hashem, your God, it is true.

Adonai Elohey-chem eh-met.
Hashem, your God, it is true.

Shabbat Shachrit (Part 1)

Track 14 **Ve'yatziv** And it is permanent

Artscroll, Expanded: Page 416, Interlinear pages 334–335.

EVERYTHING ABOUT HASHEM IS GENUINE, BEAUTIFUL AND EVERLASTING.

Veh-ya-tziyv veh-na-chon veh-ka-yam veh-ya-shar veh-neh-eh-man veh-ah-houv
And (it is) permanent and solid, and existing, and fair and steadfast, and (it is) loved

veh-cha-viyv veh-nech-mud veh-na-iym veh-nora veh-adiyr ou-meh-tou-kan
and cherished, and lovely and pleasant, and awesome and powerful, and (it is) correct,

ou-meh-kou-bal veh-tov veh-ya-feh ha-davar ha-zeh ah-ley-nou leh-oh-lam va-ed.
and accepted, and good and beautiful, this ever-lasting declaration (of faith) for us.

Eh-met Elohey oh-lam Malkeh-nou, tzour Yaakov magen yish-eh-nou,
True, the God of the world is our King, the Rock of Jacob is the Shield of our salvation,

leh-dor va-dor hou ka-yam ou-shmo ka-yam veh-chi-soh na-chon,
from (each) generation to (the next) generation He endures, and His Name endures, and His throne is solid,

ou-mal-chuto veh-eh-moun-ato la-ad ka-yeh-eh-met. Ou-dva-rav chai-yim
and His Kingdom and His faithfulness endure forever. And His words are alive

veh-ka-ya-miym, neh-eh-ma-niym veh-nech-mud-iym, la-ad ou-leh-olmey ola-miym.
and on-going, faithful and lovely, for always and forever.

Al avoteynou veh-ah-leynou al ba-neynou veh-al doro-teynou veh-al col dorot
For our forefathers, and for us, for our children, and for our generations, and for all the generations

zera Israel ava-deyh-cha.
of the seed of Israel, Your servants.

Track 15 **Al ha'rishonim** For the first

Artscroll, Expanded: Page 418, Interlinear page 336.

EVERY GENERATION HAS ALWAYS KNOWN THAT ONLY HASHEM IS OUR GOD AND KING.

Al ha-rish-oniym veh-al ha-ach-roniym davar tov veh-ka-yam leh-olam va-ed,
For the first (generations), and for (through to) the last (generations), (this) declaration (of faith) is good and endures forever and ever,

eh-met veh-eh-mouna chok veh-lo ya-avor. Eh-met sh-ata hou Adonai Eloheynou
true and steadfast, (it is) a law and it will not pass by (be abolished). It is true that it is You, Hashem, our God,

veh-Elohey avoteynou, malkeh-nou Meh-lech avoteynou goh-ah-lenou
and the God of our forefathers, (Who is) our King, King of our forefathers, our Redeemer,

goh-el avoteynou, yotz-renou tzour yeh-shu-a-tenou, poh-denou ou-matziy-lenou
Redeemer of our forefathers, our Maker, the Rock of our salvation, our Liberator, and our Rescuer;

meh-oh-lam shmeh-cha, ain Elohim zoula-teh-cha.
Your Name is from always (the very beginning of the world), there is no God other than You.

Shabbat Shachrit (Part 1)

Track 16 **Ezrat avotanu** Helper of our forefathers
Artscroll, Expanded: Pages 418–420, Interlinear pages 336–339.

HASHEM IS ALWAYS HELPING US AND BRINGS HAPPINESS INTO OUR LIVES. HASHEM PROMISED TO PROTECT ISRAEL.

Eh-zrat avoteynou ata hou meh-oh-lam magen ou-mo-shiya livney-hem achrey-hem
Helper of our forefathers, You have always been a Shield and a Savior for (all) their children (who came) after them,

beh-chol dor va-dor. Beh-roum oh-lam moshav-eh-cha ou-mish-pa-teyh-cha
in each and every generation. At the summit of the world is Your dwelling place, and Your law

veh-tzid-kat-cha ad af-sey aretz. Ah-shrey ish sh-yishma
and Your righteousness are (extend) to the ends of the earth. Happy is the man who will listen

leh-mitzvo-teyh-cha, veh-Torat-cha oud-var-cha ya-siym al li-boh.
to Your commandments, and will affix Your Torah and Your word onto his heart.

Eh-met ah-ta hou Ah-don leh-ameh-cha ou-Meh-lech gibor la-riyv riy-vam.
It is true (that) You are (the) Master for Your people, and (that You are) the Mighty King who fights their battles.

Eh-met ata hou rishon veh-ata hou ach-aron, oumi-bala-deyh-cha ain lanou Meh-lech
It is true (that) You are the first, and that You are (also) the last, and (that) other than You we have no king,

goh-el ou-mo-shiya. Mi-mitzrai-yim geh-al-tanou Adonai Eloheynou oumi-beyt
redeemer and savior. From Egypt, You redeemed us, Hashem, our God, and from the house

ava-diym pdiy-ta-nou col beh-choh-rey-hem ha-ragta, ou-veh-choh-reh-cha ga-al-ta,
of slaves You freed us, You slew all their (Egypt's) firstborn, and You redeemed Your (Israel's) firstborn,

veh-yam souf ba-ka-ata, veh-zeh-diym tiba-ata, viy-di-diym heh-eh-varta,
and You split the Sea of Reeds, and drowned the arrogant, and You brought the cherished ones (safely) across,

vai-cha-sou ma-yim tza-rey-hem, eh-chad meh-hem loh no-tar. PSALM 106:11
and (You) covered their foes with water, not even one of whom was left.

Al zot shib-chou ah-hou-viym veh-romemou El,
For this the beloved ones praised and exalted God,

veh-natnou yeh-di-diym zmi-rot shiy-rot veh-tish-ba-chot,
and the cherished ones (also) gave hymns, songs, and praises,

bra-chot veh-hoda-ot leh-Meh-lech El chai veh-ka-yam, ram veh-nisa,
blessings, and thanks to the King, the God who lives and endures, exalted and upraised,

gadol veh-nora, mash-piyl geh-iym, ou-mag-biy-ha shfa-liym, mo-tziy ah-si-riym
great and awesome, who humbles the proud, and lifts up the lowly, frees the captives,

ou-fo-deh ana-viym, veh-ozer da-liym, veh-oh-neh leh-amo beh-et sha-vam eh-lav.
and liberates the humble, and helps the poor, and answers to His people at the time they cry out to Him.

Teh-hilot leh-El el-yon barouch hou ou-meh-vorach Moshe ou-vney Israel
Laudations to the supreme God, Blessed is He, and blessed (by all); Moses and the Children of Israel

leh-cha anou shiyra, beh-sim-cha raba veh-amrou koulam.
answered You with song, with great happiness, and everyone proclaimed:

Mi kamo-cha ba-Eh-lim Adonai, mi kamo-cha neh-eh-dar ba-ko-desh,
Who is like You amongst the deities, Hashem, who is like You magnificent in holiness,

nora teh-hilot, oh-seh peh-leh. Shiyra cha-dasha shib-chou geh-ou-liym
(too) awesome for adulations, performer of wonders? With a new song, the redeemed ones praised

Shabbat Shachrit (Part 1)

leh-shim-cha al sfat ha-yam, ya-chad koulam hoh-dou veh-him-liych-ou veh-amrou:
Your Name at the sea shore, (and) all of them together gave thanks, and they made (You) Sovereign, and they said:

Adonai yim-loch leh-olam va-ed.
Hashem will reign forever and ever.

Tzour Israel, kou-ma beh-ezrat Israel, ouf-deh ki-neh-ou-meh-cha Yehuda veh-Israel.
Rock of Israel, rise up in aid of Israel, and liberate as You pledged, Judah and Israel.

Goh-ah-lenou Adonai tzva-ot shmo, keh-dosh Israel.
Our Redeemer, Hashem, (Lord) of the armies (of Israel), is His Name, the Holy One of Israel.

Barouch ata Adonai ga-al Israel.
Blessed are You, Hashem, who redeemed Israel.

THE START OF THE AMIDAH (STANDING) PRAYER
FOR SHABBAT SHACHRIT (OF THE DAWN).

WE PRAY IT FIRST AS INDIVIDUALS AND THEN WE SING IT TOGETHER.

Track 17 **Amidah 1: Baruch ata Adonai** Blessed are You, Hashem

Artscroll, Expanded: Page 420, Interlinear pages 339–341.

**HASHEM REWARDS THE GOOD DEEDS OF OUR FOREFATHERS BY HELPING US.
A REMINDER TO US TO BE GOOD PEOPLE.**

(Adonai, sa-fa-tai tif-tach ou-piy yagid teh-hila-teh-cha). Said quietly to oneself.
Hashem, open my lips and my mouth will speak Your praise (praise You).

Barouch ata Adonai Eloheynou veh-Elohey avoteynou, Elohey Avraham,
Blessed are You, Hashem, our God, and the God of our forefathers, God of Abraham,

Elohey Yitzchak, veh-Elohey Yaakov, ha-El ha-gadol ha-gibor veh-ha-nora,
God of Isaac, and God of Jacob, the God, the Great One, the Mighty One, and the Awesome One,

El el-yon, goh-mel chasa-diym tov-iym veh-ko-neh ha-col, veh-zo-cher
the supreme God, who gives back (to us) loving kindnesses that are good, and creates everything, and remembers

chas-dey ah-vot, ou-meh-viy goh-el livney bney-hem,
the loving kindnesses of the forefathers, and brings a redeemer to the children of their children,

leh-ma-an shmo beh-ah-hava.
for the sake of His Name, with love.

Meh-lech ozer ou-mo-shiya ou-magen. Barouch ata Adonai magen Avraham.
The King who helps, and saves and defends. Blessed are You, Hashem, Shield of Abraham.

Ata gibor leh-oh-lam Adonai, meh-cha-yeh metiym ata, rav leh-ho-shiya.
You are mighty forever Hashem, You resurrect the dead, You can save in abundance.

(Ma-shiyv ha-rou-ach ou-mo-riyd ha-geshem). Only said between Simchat Torah and Pesach (the winter months).
(You who makes the wind blow and the rain fall).

Shabbat Shachrit (Part 1)

Track 18 **Amidah 1: Mechalkel chaim** He nourishes the living

Artscroll, Expanded: Page 420, Interlinear page 341.

HASHEM PROTECTS ALL OF US ESPECIALLY THE WEAK AND NEEDY.

Meh-chal-kel chai-yim beh-cheh-sed, meh-cha-yeh metiym beh-rach-amiym rabiym,
He nourishes the living with loving kindness, He revives the dead with abundant mercies,

soh-mech nof-liym, veh-rofeh choh-liym, ou-ma-tiyr ah-sou-riym, ou-meh-ka-yem
He supports the fallen, and He cures the ill, and He frees the captives, and He keeps

eh-mou-nato li-yesh-eney a-farr. Mi kamo-cha ba-al gvou-rot, ou-mi doh-meh lach,
His faith to those sleeping in the dust. Who is like You, Master of mighty deeds, and who is similar to You,

Meh-lech meh-miyt ou-meh-cha-yeh ou-matz-miy-ach yeh-shoua.
the King who determines death and restores life, and makes salvation sprout?

Veh-neh-eh-man ata leh-hach-yot meh-tiym.
And You are faithful to revive the dead.

Barouch ata Adonai meh-cha-yeh ha-metiym.
Blessed are You, Hashem, resurrector of the dead.

Shabbat Shachrit (Part 1)

Track 19 **Amidah 1: Nekadesh** We will sanctify

Artscroll, Expanded: Page 422, Interlinear pages 342–343.

WE WANT TO SEE HASHEM'S HONOR EVERYWHERE IN HOLY JERUSALEM AND WITNESS HIS REIGN IN ZION, HIS ETERNAL KINGDOM, ISRAEL.

Neh-ka-desh et shim-cha ba-oh-lam keh-shem
We will sanctify Your Name in the world, (just) as they (the angels)

sh-mak-di-shiym oh-toh bi-shmey marom,
sanctify it in the heavens up high;

ka-ka-touv al yad neviy-eh-cha, veh-kara zeh el zeh veh-amar:
as it is written by the hand of Your prophets, (one angel) would call the other (angel) and say:

Kadosh kadosh kadosh Adonai tzeh-va-ot, meh-lo col ha-aretz keh-vo-doh.
Holy, holy, holy is Hashem, (Lord) of the armies (of Israel), the whole earth (land) is filled with His honor (glory).

Az beh-kol ra-ash gadol ah-diyr veh-cha-zak mash-mi-iym kol,
Then with a sound, a noise (that is) great, powerful and loud, they make (their) voice(s) heard,

mit-nas-iym leh-oumat sra-fiym, leh-ou-ma-tam barouch yomerou:
they raise themselves up (so as) to face the Seraphim angels, (once) facing them they proclaim, Blessed:

Barouch kvod Adonai mim-komo.
Blessed is the honor (glory) of Hashem from His place.

Mim-kom-cha malkeh-nou toh-fiy-a, veh-timloch ah-leynou,
From Your place, our King, (may You) appear and rule over us,

ki meh-cha-kiym ah-nachnou lach.
because we are waiting for You.

Matai tim-loch beh-tZi-yon, beh-karov beh-ya-mey-nou, leh-olam va-ed tish-kon:
When will You reign in Zion? Shortly (soon please) in our days, dwell there forever and ever.

Tit-ga-dal veh-tit-ka-dash beh-toch Yeru-sha-lai-yim iyr-cha, leh-dor va-dor
May You be magnified and sanctified inside Jerusalem, Your city, from generation to (the next) generation,

ou-leh-netzach netza-chiym.
and for all eternity (and) eternities.

Veh-eyney-nou tir-ey-na malchou-teh-cha, ka-davar* ha-ah-mour
And may our eyes see Your Kingdom, as this matter is expressed,

beh-shiy-rey ou-zeh-cha, al yedey David meshiy-ach tzid-keh-cha:
in the songs of Your might, (composed) by the hand of (King) David, Your righteous anointed one:

PSALM 146:10
<u>Yimloch Adonai leh-olam, Elo-hai-yich tZi-yon leh-dor va-dor halleluya.</u>
Hashem will reign forever, your God, O Zion, from generation to (the next) generation, Halleluya.

Leh-dor va-dor na-giyd godd-leh-cha ou-leh-netzach netza-chiym
From generation to (the next) generation, we will talk (about) Your greatness, and for all eternity (and) eternities,

kedoush-at-cha nak-diysh, veh-shiv-cheh-cha Elo-heynou mi-piy-nou
we will sanctify Your holiness, and praise for You, our God, from our mouth

lo ya-moush leh-olam va-ed, ki El Meh-lech gadol veh-ka-dosh ata.
will never ever cease, because You are a great and holy God (and) King.

Barouch ata Adonai, ha-El ha-kadosh.
Blessed are You, Hashem, the God who is holy.

* Alternatively: as this (place of) order is expressed...

Shabbat Shachrit (Part 1)

Track 20 **Amidah 1: Yismach Moshe, Ve'shamru, Ve'lo netato**
Moses was happy, And they will guard, & He did not give

Artscroll, Expanded: Page 424, Interlinear pages 344–346.

MOSES WAS HAPPY TO BE HASHEM'S MESSENGER.

Yis-mach Moshe beh-matnat chel-ko, ki eh-ved neh-eh-man ka-ra-ta lo.
Moses was happy with the gift of his portion (and) because You called him a faithful servant.

Kliyl tif-eh-ret beh-rosho na-tata lo, beh-omdo leh-fa-neyh-cha al har Sinai.
You (gave him) placed on his head, a crown of splendor, when he stood before You on Mount Sinai.

Ou-shney lou-chot ava-niym hoh-riyd beh-yado, veh-ka-touv ba-hem
And he brought down two tablets of stone in his hand, and inscribed on them

shmiy-rat Shabbat, veh-chen ka-touv beh-Torah-teh-cha:
(was the commandment) to observe (guard) the Shabbat, and so this is written in Your Torah:

THE SHABBAT DAY IS AN ETERNAL PACT BETWEEN HASHEM AND ISRAEL.

Veh-shamrou bney Israel et ha-Shabbat, la-asot et ha-Shabbat leh-doro-tam
And the Children of Israel will guard the Shabbat, (and will) observe the Shabbat throughout their generations,

briyt oh-lam. Beyni ou-veyn bney Israel ot hiy leh-oh-lam, ki sh-shet ya-miym
as an eternal covenant. Between Me and the Children of Israel, it is an eternal sign, because in six days

asa Adonai et ha-shamai-yim veh-et ha-aretz, ou-va-yom ha-shvi-iy shavat
Hashem made the heaven(s) and the earth, and on the seventh day, He rested

va-yinafash.
and was refreshed.

THE SHABBAT DAY IS A GIFT OF LOVE FROM HASHEM TO THE JEWISH PEOPLE.

Veh-lo neh-tato Adonai Eloheynou leh-goh-yey ha-ara-tzot,
And Hashem, our God, did not give (the Shabbat) to the (other) nations of the (rest of) the earth (lands),

veh-lo hin-chal-toh malkeh-nou leh-ovdey psi-iliym, veh-gam bim-nou-cha-toh
and our King did not bequeath it to idol worshippers, and (therefore) also in its restful tranquility,

lo yish-kenou ar-eh-liym. Ki leh-Israel am-cha neh-tato beh-ah-hava,
the uncircumcised will not reside. Because to Israel, Your people, You gave it with love,

leh-zera Yaakov ah-sher bam ba-char-ta. Am meh-kad-shey shvi-iy, kou-lam
to the seed of Jacob whom You chose. The people who sanctify the seventh (day) will all

yisbeh-ou veh-yit-an-gou mi-touv-eh-cha, ouva-shvi-iy ra-tziyta bo veh-ki-dashto,
be satisfied, and will delight from Your goodness, and You favored (coveted) the seventh (day) and sanctified it,

chemdat ya-miym oto ka-ra-ta, zeh-cher leh-ma-a-seh beh-reh-shiyt.
You called it the most desired of days, a remembrance of the (Your) Act of Creation (of the world).

Track 21 Amidah 1: Elohanu Our God

Artscroll, Expanded: Page 424, Interlinear pages 346–347.

PLEASE HASHEM BLESS US WITH YOUR GOODNESS SO WE CAN BECOME BETTER PEOPLE.

Elo-heynou veh-Elohey avo-teynou, reh-tzeh bim-noucha-tenou.
Our God, and the God of our forefathers, (please) find favor in our rest.

Kad-shenou beh-mitzvo-teyh-cha, veh-ten chel-kenou beh-Torah-teh-cha. Sab-enou
Make us holy with Your commandments and (please) give us our place (heritage/birthright) in Your Torah. Satisfy us

mi-tou-veh-cha, veh-samm-chen-ou bi-yeshoua-teh-cha, veh-ta-herr li-benou
with Your goodness, and make us happy in Your salvation, and purify our heart(s)

leh-ov-deh-cha beh-eh-met. Veh-han-chiy-lenou Adonai Eloheynou
to serve You with sincerity. And bequeath to us, Hashem, our God,

beh-ah-hava ou-veh-ratzon Shabbat kod-sh-cha, veh-ya-nou-chou bo Israel
with love and with favor, Your holy Shabbat, and Israel will rest on it,

meh-kad-shey shmeh-cha. Barouch ata Adonai, meh-ka-desh ha-Shabbat.
the sanctifiers of Your Name. Blessed are You, Hashem, who sanctifies the Shabbat.

Track 22 Amidah 1: Retze, & Ve'techezeyna
Find favor, & May we witness

Artscroll, Expanded: Page 426, Interlinear pages 347–348.

WE ARE ASKING HASHEM TO REBUILD HIS HOLY TEMPLE IN JERUSALEM.
WE WANT TO SHOW HASHEM OUR LOVE.

Reh-tzeh Adonai Eloheynou beh-am-cha Israel ouvi-tfila-tam, veh-ha-shev
Hashem, our God, find favor in Your people Israel and in their prayer, and return

et ha-avoda li-dviyr beyt-eh-cha
the worship to the (rebuilt) sanctuary of Your Temple (in Jerusalem),

veh-ishey Israel ou-teh-fi-la-tam beh-ah-hava teh-kabel
and accept the fire-offerings and prayer of Israel with love

beh-ratzon, ou-teh-hiy leh-ratzon ta-miyd avodat Israel am-eh-cha.
and favor, and may the worship of Israel, Your people, always be appealing (to You).

Veh-teh-cheh-zeyh-na ey-ney-nou beh-shouv-cha leh-tZi-yon beh-rach-amiym.
And may our eyes witness Your return to Zion in compassion.

Barouch ata Adonai, ha-mach-ziyr shchiyn-ah-toh leh-tZi-yon.
Blessed are You, Hashem, who restores His divine presence to Zion.

Shabbat Shachrit (Part 1)

Track 23 **Amidah 1: Modim** Thanks

Artscroll, Expanded: Pages 426–428, Interlinear pages 348–351.

WE THANK HASHEM FOR ALL THE WONDERFUL THINGS THAT ARE WITH US AT ALL TIMES. IT IS IMPORTANT TO BE AWARE OF AND GRATEFUL FOR EVERY BLESSING THAT WE HAVE.

Moh-diym ah-nachnou lach, sh-ata hou Adonai Eloheynou veh-Elohey avoteynou
We thank You, that it is You who is Hashem, our God, and the God of our forefathers,

leh-oh-lam va-ed. Tzour chai-yeynou, magen yish-enou, ata hou leh-dor va-dor.
for all eternity. Rock of our lives, Shield of our salvation, it is You from generation to (the next) generation.

Noh-deh leh-cha oun-sa-perr teh-hila-teh-cha al chai-yeynou hamm-sou-riym
We will thank You and we will verbalize Your praise, for our lives that are committed

beh-yad-eh-cha, veh-al nish-moh-teynou hap-koudot lach, veh-al ni-seyh-cha
into Your hand, and for our souls that are entrusted to You, and for Your miracles

sh-beh-chol yom ima-nou, veh-al nif-leh-oteyh-cha veh-tovo-teyh-cha sh-beh-chol et,
that are with us every day, and for Your wonders and Your favors that are (with us) at all time(s),

eh-rev va-bo-ker veh-tzo-hoh-ra-yim. Ha-tov ki lo ka-lou rach-ah-meyh-cha,
evening, and morning and afternoon. (You are) the Good One because (as) Your mercy never depletes,

veh-hamm-ra-chem ki lo tamou chasa-deyh-cha, meh-oh-lam ki-viy-nou lach.
and the Merciful One, because (as) Your loving kindnesses never end, our hope has always been to You.

Veh-al koulam yit-barach veh-yit-romam shim-cha mal-kenou tamiyd
And for all of these (things) may Your Name, our King, be continuously blessed and exalted,

leh-oh-lam va-ed.
forever and ever.

Veh-chol ha-chai-yim yoh-dou-cha selah, vi-yeh-ha-lelou et shim-cha beh-eh-met.
And all that is alive will give gratitude to You forever, and will praise Your Name with sincerity.

Ha-El yeh-shoua-tenou veh-ezra-tenou selah.
The God of our salvation and of our succor, forever.

Barouch ata Adonai ha-tov shim-cha ou-leh-cha na-eh leh-ho-dot.
Blessed are You, Hashem, the Good One is Your Name, and to You it is fitting to give thanks.

Shabbat Shachrit (Part 1)

Track 24 **Amidah 1: Elohanu v'Elohai avotanu barchanu, & Sim Shalom**
Our God and God of our forefathers bless us, & Establish peace

Artscroll, Expanded: Pages 428–430, Interlinear pages 352–353.

PLEASE HASHEM, BLESS US LIKE THE KOHANIM (PRIESTS) BLESSED OUR ANCESTORS IN THE HOLY TEMPLE OF JERUSALEM.

Eloheynou veh-Elohey avo-teynou bar-chen-ou ba-bra-cha ha-meh-shou-leh-shet
Our God, and the God of our forefathers, bless us with the triple (three verse) blessing

ba-Torah, hak-touva al yedey Moshe av-deh-cha, ha-ah-moura mi-pi Aharon
in the Torah, written by the hand of Moses Your servant, (and) as spoken from the mouth of Aaron

ou-va-nav, Koha-niym am kedosh-eh-cha ka-amour.
and his sons, the Priests, Your holy people, as it is said:

Yeh-va-rech-eh-cha Adonai veh-yish-meh-reh-cha.
May Hashem bless you and protect you.

Ya-er Adonai pa-nav eh-leyh-cha viy-chou-neh-ka.
May Hashem light up His face towards you, and be gracious to you.

Yi-sah Adonai pa-nav eh-leyh-cha, veh-ya-sem leh-cha shalom.
May Hashem turn His face towards you, and establish peace for you.

WE ASK HASHEM TO BLESS HIS PEOPLE ISRAEL WITH PEACE, THE GREATEST BLESSING OF ALL.

Siym shalom toh-va ouv-ra-cha, chen va-cheh-sed veh-rach-amiym ah-leynou
Establish peace, goodness, and blessing, grace, and loving kindness and mercies on us,

veh-al col Israel ah-meh-cha. Bar-chen-ou aviy-nou, kou-lanou keh-eh-chad beh-orr
and on all Israel, Your people. Bless us, our Father, all of us as one (single person), with the light

pan-eyh-cha, ki beh-orr pan-eyh-cha na-ta-ta la-nou, Adonai Eloheynou,
of Your face, because through the light of Your face, You gave us, Hashem, our God,

Torat chai-yim veh-ah-ha-vat cheh-sed outz-daka, ouv-ra-cha, veh-ra-cha-miym,
the Torah of Life, and (through Her) a love for loving kindness, and charity, and blessing, and compassion,

veh-chai-yim, veh-shalom. Veh-tov beh-ey-neyh-cha leh-va-rech et am-cha Israel
and life, and peace. And may it be (it is) good in Your eyes to bless, Your people, Israel,

beh-chol et ou-veh-chol sha-ah bi-shlom-eh-cha.
at every time, and at every hour, with Your peace.

Barouch ata Adonai, ha-meh-va-rech et amo Israel ba-shalom
Blessed are You, Hashem, who blesses His people, Israel, with peace

(et amo Israel ba-shalom).
(His people, Israel, with peace).

END OF THE (REPETITION OF THE) SHACHRIT AMIDAH.

Shabbat Shachrit (Part 1)

Track 25 **Yitgadal, No 1 Full Kaddish**

Artscroll, Expanded: Pages 430–432, Interlinear pages 355–357.

FIRST OF 2 IN SHABBAT MORNING SERVICE.

HASHEM, PLEASE ACCEPT THE PRAYERS OF THE WHOLE HOUSE OF ISRAEL, FOR LIFE AND PEACE.

Yit-gadal veh-yit-kadash shmeh raba. Beh-olma di bra kir-ou-teh
May His great Name be magnified and sanctified. In the world that He created as He wanted it,

veh-yamliych malchou-teh, beh-chai-yey-chon ou-veh-yo-mey-chon ouv-chai-yey
may His Kingship reign, in your lifetimes, and in your days, and in the lifetimes

deh-chol bet Israel, ba-agala ou-vizman ka-riyv. Veh-imrou amen.
of all of the House of Israel, speedily and soon. And we say: Amen.

Yeh-heh shmeh raba meh-vo-rach leh-oh-lam ou-leh-olmey olmai-ya.
May His great Name be blessed forever, and for all eternity.

Yit-barach veh-yishtabach veh-yitpa-ar veh-yitromam veh-yitna-seh veh-yit-hadar
Blessed, and praised, and glorified, and exalted, and upraised, and honored,

veh-yit-ah-leh veh-yit-ha-lal shmeh deh-koudsha briych hou.
and elevated, and extolled, is the Name of the Holy One, Blessed is He.

Leh-elah min col bir-cha-ta veh-shiy-rata toush-beh-cha-ta veh-neh-cheh-mata
Way above any blessing, and song, praise, and cheer

da-amiy-ran beh-olma. Veh-imrou amen.
that are vocalized in the world, and we say: Amen.

Titkabel tzlot-hon ouva-oute-hon deh-chol bet Israel ka-dam avou-hon
(Please) accept the prayers and (humble) appeals, of the whole House of Israel, (placed) before their Father

di bishmai-ya. Veh-imrou amen.
in heaven. And we say: Amen.

Yeh-heh shlama raba min shmai-ya, veh-chai-yim ah-leynou veh-al col Israel.
May there be abundant peace from heaven, and life for us and for all Israel.

Veh-imrou amen.
And we say: Amen.

Oseh shalom bimro-mav, hou ya-aseh shalom ah-leynou, veh-al col Israel.
He who makes peace in His heights, may He make peace for us and for all Israel.

Veh-imrou amen.
And we say: Amen

> **THE LEAD UP TO THE OPENING OF THE HOLY ARK STARTS NOW.**

Track 26 **Ain kamocha** There is nothing like You

Artscroll, Expanded: Page 432, Interlinear pages 357–358.

HASHEM IS THE RULER OVER EVERYTHING.
PLEASE HASHEM, GIVE YOUR PEOPLE STRENGTH AND BLESS ISRAEL WITH PEACE.

Ain ka-mo-cha ba-Elohim Adonai, veh-ain keh-ma-a-seyh-cha. Mal-choute-cha, ^{PSALM 86:8}
There is nothing amongst the deities like You, Hashem, and nothing like Your deeds. Your Kingdom

mal-choute col ola-miym, ou-memshal-teh-cha beh-chol dor va-dor, ^{PSALM 145:13}
is sovereign for all eternity, and Your dominion is for every generation and generation.

Adonai meh-lech, Adonai ma-lach, Adonai yim-loch, leh-oh-lam va-ed.
Hashem reigns, Hashem reigned, Hashem will reign, forever and ever.

Adonai oz leh-amo yi-ten, Adonai yeh-varech et amo ba-shalom. ^{PSALM 29:11}
Hashem will give strength to His nation, Hashem will bless His people with peace.

Av ha-rach-amiym hey-tiyva bir-tzon-cha et tZi-yon,
Father of mercies, do good, as is Your will, to Zion,

tiv-neh choh-mot Yerusha-lai-yim. ^{PSALM 51:20}
(and re-)build Jerusalem's walls.

Ki beh-cha leh-vad ba-tach-nou, Meh-lech El ram veh-nisah, Ah-don ola-miym.
For in You alone do we trust, O King, God, exalted and upraised, Master of (all the) worlds.

Shabbat Shachrit (Part 1)

> **THE HOLY ARK IS NOW OPENED.**

Track 27 **Vayehi binsoah** And as it (the Holy Ark) travelled
Artscroll, Expanded: Page 432, Interlinear pages 358–359.

MOSES SAID THAT WHEN THE HOLY ARK WAS TRAVELLING IN THE DESERT IT WAS PROTECTING THE JEWISH PEOPLE FROM THEIR ENEMIES.

Vai-hiy binsoh-ah ha-aron va-yo-mer Moshe, kouma Adonai
And as the (Holy) Ark (of the Covenant) travelled (in the desert), Moses would say; Rise up, Hashem,

veh-ya-fou-tzou oiy-veyh-cha veh-ya-nou-sou meh-san-eyh-cha mi-pan-eyh-cha.
and Your enemies will scatter, and Your haters will flee from before You.

Ki mi-tZi-yon teh-tzeh Torah, (ki mi-tZi-yon teh-tzeh Torah),
Because from Zion will set out (come) the Torah, (because from Zion will set out (come) the Torah),

ou-dvar Adonai mi-Yeru-sha-lai-yim.
and the word of Hashem, from Jerusalem.

Barouch sh-natan Torah leh-amo Israel bik-dou-sha-toh.
Blessed is He who gave the Torah, to His people Israel, in His holiness.

Track 28 **Brich shmai** Blessed is the Name

Artscroll, Expanded: Page 436, Interlinear pages 362–364.

**EACH OF US WANTS TO BE WORTHY IN HASHEM'S EYES.
WE PRAY THAT HASHEM PROTECTS US AND ISRAEL.**

Briych shmeh deh-mareh olma, briych kit-rach veh-at-rach. Yeh-heh reh-ou-tach
Blessed is the Name of the Master of the world, blessed is Your crown and Your place. May Your favor

im am-ach Israel leh-oh-lam, ou-foor-kan yemiy-nach acha-zey leh-am-ach
forever be with Your people Israel, and may the salvation of Your right (hand) be on display to Your people

beh-veyt makdesh-ach, ou-leh-am-tou-yey la-na mi-touv neh-hoh-rach,
in Your holy Temple, and may the goodness of Your light extend to us,

ou-leh-kabel tzlot-ana beh-rach-amiyn. Yeh-heh ra-ava ka-da-mach, deh-toh-riych lan
and may our prayers be accepted with compassion. May it be Your will, that You prolong for us

chai-yin beh-tiyv-ou-ta, veh-leh-heh-vey ana pkiy-da beh-goh tzadiy-ka-ya,
lives of (in) goodness, and that I be counted amongst the righteous,

leh-mir-cham alai ou-leh-mintar ya-ti veh-yat col di li, veh-diyl am-ach Israel.
(so that You) have mercy on me, and protect me, and all that is mine, and (all that) which is (belongs) to, Your people, Israel.

Annt hou zan leh-chola ou-meh-farness leh-chola, annt hou sha-liyt al cola. Annt hou
It is You who feeds everybody, and provides to everybody, it is You who rules over everything. It is You

deh-sha-liyt al mal-cha-ya, ou-mal-chou-ta diy-lach hiy. Ana avda deh-koud-sha
who rules over kings, and the Kingship is Yours. I am a servant of the Holy One,

briych hou, deh-sa-giyd-nah kameh oumi-kama diy-kar oraiy-teh beh-chol
Blessed is He, I prostrate myself before Him, and before the glory of His Torah, at all

idan veh-idan. Lo al eh-nosh ra-chiytz-nah, veh-lo al bar Elohin sa-miych-na,
times and moments. I do not place my trust in (any) man, and nor do I rely on (any) angel,

eh-la beh-Elo-ha di-shmai-ya, deh-hou Elo-ha kshott, veh-oh-raiy-teh kshott,
rather solely (all my trust is) in the God in heaven, who is the God of truth, and His Torah is truth,

ou-neh-viy-oh-hiy kshott, ou-masgeh leh-meh-eh-badd ta-veh-van ou-kshott.
and His prophets are truth, and He abundantly acts with goodness and truth.

Beh ana ra-chiytz, veh-lish-meh ka-diysha ya-kiyra ana eh-mar toush-beh-chan.
I trust in Him, and to His holy and glorious Name, I proclaim praises.

Yeh-heh ra-ava ka-da-mach deh-tif-tach liba-iy beh-oh-raiy-ta, veh-tash-liym
May it be Your will that You open my heart to the Torah, and that You fulfill

mish-ah-liyn deh-li-ba-iy, veh-liba deh-chol am-ach Israel, leh-tav oul-chai-yin
the requests of my heart, and (the requests) of the heart of all Your people, Israel, for goodness, and for life

veh-lish-lam.
and for peace.

Shabbat Shachrit (Part 1)

> THE HOLY TORAH IS NOW TAKEN OUT OF THE HOLY ARK AND HANDED
> TO THE PRAYER LEADER. THE HOLY ARK IS THEN CLOSED.

Track 29 Shma Israel, Gadlu, Al hacol, & Av ha'rachamim

Hear O Israel, Declare the Greatness, For everything, & Father of Compassion

Artscroll, Expanded: Pages 436–438, Interlinear pages 364–367.

> THE PRAYER LEADER HOLDS THE HOLY TORAH AND SINGS OUT TO REMIND US
> THE REASON FOR JUDAISM AND WHY IT EXISTS.

SHMA ISRAEL ADONAI ELOHEYNOU, ADONAI EH-CHAD.
Hear O Israel, Hashem is our God, Hashem is one.

EH-CHAD HOU ELOHEYNOU, GADOL ADONEYNOU, KADOSH SHMO.
Our God is one, our Master is great, His Name is holy.

> THE PRAYER LEADER BOWS TO THE HOLY ARK,
> AND THEN TURNS TO US AND SINGS.

GADLOU LA-ADONAI ITI OU-NEH-ROMEMA SHMO YACH-DAV. *PSALM 34:4*
Declare the greatness of Hashem with me, and together we will exalt His Name.

> THE HOLY TORAH IS CARRIED TO THE BIMAH (PRAYER TABLE).
> WE SALUTE HASHEM'S HOLY NAME IN SONG.
> WE PRAY FOR HASHEM'S RETURN TO ZION, HIS HOME ISRAEL.

Leh-cha Adonai hag-dou-lah veh-ha-gvoura veh-ha-tif-eh-ret veh-ha-netz-ach
To You, Hashem, is the greatness, and the might, and the splendor, and the victory

veh-ha-hod ki col ba-sha-mai-yim ou-va-aretz, leh-cha Adonai ha-mamm-la-cha
and the majesty, because (as) everything in the heaven(s) and the earth (is Yours), Hashem Yours is the Kingdom

veh-ha-mit-na-seh leh-chol leh-rosh. Romemou Adonai Elo-heynou,
and the supremacy over every leader. Exalt Hashem, our God,

veh-hish-tach-avou la-ha-dom ra-glav, kadosh hou. Romemou Adonai Eloheynou, *PSALM 99:5*
and bow down to His footstool, (for) He is holy. Exalt Hashem, our God,

veh-hish-tach-avou leh-har kodsho, ki kadosh Adonai Eloheynou. *PSALM 99:9*
and bow down to the Mountain of His Holiness (in Jerusalem), because Hashem, our God, is holy.

Shabbat Shachrit (Part 1)

Al ha-col, yitga-dal veh-yitka-dash veh-yish-ta-bach veh-yitpa-ar veh-yitro-mamm
For everything, may it (His Name) be magnified, and sanctified, and praised, and glorified, and exalted,

veh-yit-na-seh shmo shel Meh-lech mal-chey hamm-la-chiym ha-ka-dosh barouch
and upraised, His Name, that of the King, King of the kings, the Holy One, Blessed

hou, ba-ola-mot sh-bara, ha-olam ha-zeh veh-ha-olam ha-ba, kir-tzono veh-chirtz-on
is He, in the worlds that He created - this world and the world to come – as He wanted, and as wanted

yeh-reh-av, veh-chirtz-on col beyt Israel. Tzour ha-ola-miym, Adon col ha-bri-yot,
by those who fear Him, and as wanted by all of the House of Israel. Rock of the worlds, Master of all the creatures,

Eloha col ha-neh-fa-shot, ha-yo-shev beh-mer-cha-vey marom, ha-shoh-chen
God of all souls, He who sits in the expanses of the heights, He who dwells

bi-shmey shmey kedem. Kedoush-ato al ha-cha-yot, ouk-doush-ato al ki-seh
in the earliest heaven of heavens. His holiness is above the Chayot angels, and His holiness is on the Throne

ha-ka-vod. Ouv-chen yit-kadash shim-cha banou, Adonai Eloheynou leh-eyney
of Glory. And so, Your Name will be sanctified within us, Hashem, our God, in the eyes (full view)

col chai. Veh-nomar leh-fa-nav shiyr cha-dash, ka-katouv: <u>shiyr-ou leh-Elohim</u>
of all that is living. And so we will vocalize a new song before Him, as it is written: Sing to God,
PSALM 68:5

<u>zamrou shmo, solou la-ro-chev ba-aravot beh-Ya shmo, veh-ilzou leh-fa-nav.</u>
make music for His Name, extol He who rides (up there) in the heavens, His Name is Yah, and rejoice before Him.

Veh-nir-eh-hou ai-yin beh-ai-yin beh-shou-vo el na-veh-hou, ka-ka-touv:
And we will see Him, eye to eye (before our eyes), on His return to His dwelling place, as it is written:

Ki ai-yin beh-ai-yin yir-ou beh-shouv Adonai tZi-yon.
For they will see, eye to eye (before their eyes), when Hashem returns to Zion.

Veh-neh-eh-mar veh-nigla kvod Adonai, veh-ra-ou col basar yach-dav ki pi
And it is said: And (so) the glory of Hashem will be revealed, and all flesh (people), together, will see that the mouth

Adonai diber.
of Hashem has spoken.

Av ha-rach-amiym hou yeh-ra-chem am amou-siym, veh-yizkor
Father of compassion, may He have mercy on the nation borne by Him, and may He remember

briyt eytan-iym, veh-ya-tziyl nafshoh-teynou min ha-sha-ot ha-ra-ot,
the covenant with the (spiritually) strong (the Patriarchs), and may He rescue our souls from the bad hours,

veh-yig-ar beh-yeh-tzer ha-ra min ha-neh-sou-iym, veh-ya-chon ot-anou
and may He remove the evil inclination from within those (people) carried by Him, and may He pardon us

lif-ley-tat ola-miym, vi-yem-aleh mi-shel-oh-teynou,
with eternal deliverance, and may He fulfil our requests,

beh-mida tova yeshua veh-rach-a-miym.
in good measure, with salvation and mercies.

Shabbat Shachrit (Part 1)

KRIAT HA-TORAH
READING OF THE TORAH

The weekly Shabbat Torah reading is called the Parasha* or Sidra**.

The yearly cycle of 54 Parashot covers all five books of Moses, our Holy Torah.

The Holy Torah is placed on the bimah. The prayer leader unrolls it, and recites a prayer calling up the Oleh – the person who "rises up" to the Torah specifically for a particular section of that week's Parasha.

This is called "getting an Aliyah" and it is an honor. The Oleh needs to be wearing a talit (prayer shawl).

The first Oleh called up by the prayer leader is always a Cohen***, assuming one is present. The Oleh's hebrew name and the hebrew name of their father is always used for every Aliyah. If no Cohen is present, then a Levite (Levi) or Israelite is called up instead.

The congregation and prayer leader then recite a very short blessing acknowledging, that it is thanks to Hashem, that we are all alive today.

There are a total of seven Aliyot "rising up's" to the Torah, sequentially, one for each section of the Parasha to be read, so seven different Oleh's, every Shabbat.

The person actually reading the Parasha section, called the Ba'al Koreh (Master Reader), then points to the starting point of the section to be read, the Oleh touches it with the tzitzit (fringes) of his talit and kisses the tzitzit.

The Oleh then stands in front of the Torah, grabs the scroll handle on each side and recites a blessing; which blesses Hashem for having chosen to give the Jewish people His Holy Torah.

The Ba'al Koreh, with the Oleh standing beside him, now reads the specific section. When the reading is finished, the Oleh touches (with the tzitzit) where the reading ended, kisses the tzitzit, and recites a blessing; which blesses Hashem for having given us the Torah of truth.

The Oleh then moves to the other side of the bimah until the end of the next Parasha section reading, and then goes back to sit down.

This is repeated a further six times, once for each Oleh.

* Parasha means; portion, section, separation, matter or topic.
** Sidra or sedra actually means the order, arrangement. In this case, of the weekly Shabbat readings.
*** Cohen or Kohen is the Hebrew word for "priest", so a Cohen is a descendant from Aaron (brother of Moses) and his Kohanim, who were the priests who served in the Holy Temple of Jerusalem. A Levi is a descendant from the Levite tribe who were given the honor, by Hashem, of assisting the Kohanim. An Israelite is a Jew who is neither a Cohen nor a Levi, basically tribe unknown.

> **PRAYERS NOW RESUME AS TORAH READINGS ARE COMPLETED.**

Track 30 Yitgadal, No 2 Half Kaddish

Artscroll, Expanded: Page 444, Interlinear page 376.

SECOND OF 3 IN SHABBAT MORNING SERVICE.
HASHEM IS WAY ABOVE ANY BLESSING, SONG OR PRAISE.

Yitgadal veh-yit-kadash shmeh raba. Beh-olma di bra kir-ou-teh
May His great Name be magnified and sanctified. In the world that He created as He wanted it,

veh-yamliych malchou-teh, beh-chai-yey-chon ou-veh-yo-meychon ouv-chai-yey
may His Kingship reign, in your lifetimes, and in your days, and in the lifetimes

deh-chol bet Israel, ba-agala ouvi-zman ka-riyv. Veh-imrou amen.
of all of the House of Israel, speedily and soon. And we say: Amen

Yeh-heh shmeh raba meh-vo-rach leh-oh-lam ou-leh-olmey olmai-ya.
May His great Name be blessed forever, and for all eternity.

Yit-barach veh-yishtabach veh-yitpa-ar veh-yitromam veh-yitna-seh veh-yit-hadar
Blessed, and praised, and glorified, and exalted, and upraised, and honored,

veh-yit-ah-leh veh-yit-ha-lal shmeh deh-koud-sha briych hou.
and elevated, and extolled, is the Name of the Holy One, Blessed is He.

Leh-elah min col bir-cha-ta veh-shiy-rata, toush-beh-cha-ta veh-neh-cheh-mata
Way above any blessing, and song, praise, and cheer

da-amiyran beh-olma. Veh-imrou amen.
that are vocalized in the world. And we say: Amen

> **IN SOME CONGREGATIONS, THE MAFTIR (CONCLUDER)**
> **PORTION OF THE TORAH READING IS REPEATED NOW.**

Shabbat Shachrit (Part 1)

> # HAGBAHA*
> THE HOLY TORAH IS LIFTED UP HIGH FOR ALL TO SEE.
> WE SING TO PROCLAIM OUR FAITH IN HASHEM.

Track 31 V'zot ha'Torah And this is the Torah
Artscroll, Expanded: Page 444, Interlinear page 377.

VEH-ZOT HA-TORAH AH-SHER SAMM MOSHE LIF-NEY BNEY ISRAEL,
And this is the Torah that Moses placed before the Children of Israel,

AL PI ADONAI BEH-YAD MOSHE.
from the mouth of Hashem, in (through) the hand of Moses.

Track 32 Etz chaim he She is the tree of life
Artscroll, Expanded: Page 444, Interlinear pages 377–378.

THE HOLY TORAH IS FULL OF GOODNESS, TEACHING US TO DO
GOOD DEEDS AND TO BE PLEASANT TO ONE ANOTHER.
WE RECOGNISE THE IMPORTANCE OF A SOLID FOUNDATION AND SOUND JUDGEMENT.

Etz chai-yim hiy la-ma-cha-zi-kiym bah, veh-tom-chay-ha meh-ou-shar.
She is the tree of life for those who grasp Her, and Her supporters (devotees) are happy (fortunate).

Dra-chay-ha dar-chey no-am veh-chol netiy-vo-tay-ha shalom.
Her ways are the ways of pleasantness, and all Her pathways are to peace.

Oh-rech ya-miym bi-miyna, bi-smola osher veh-cha-vod.
Longevity (lengthy days) are on Her right, on Her left is wealth (plenty) and dignity.

Adonai cha-fetz leh-ma-an tzid-ko yag-diyl Torah veh-ya-a-diyr.
Hashem wanted, for the sake of His (and Israel's) righteousness, to make the Torah great and magnificent (powerful).

> # GLILA*
> THE HOLY TORAH IS NOW ROLLED UP, SECURED WITH A BELT,
> COVERED WITH A VELVET CLOAK, AND ADORNED WITH
> A SILVER CROWN, BREAST PLATE AND POINTER ROD.
> THE TORAH IS NOT TAKEN BACK TO THE ARK YET.

* Hagbaha means "raising", performed by the Magbiha "raiser".

** Glila means "rolling", performed by the Golel "roller".

It is an honor to be called up to be the Magbiha or Golel.

HAFTARA
READING FROM THE PROPHETS

The reading of the weekly Haftara* portion, each of which are selected passages from the Prophets, follows immediately after the Torah reading is completed.

Only a select number of passages, from the Prophets, make up the fixed yearly Shabbat Haftara cycle.

The weekly Haftara portion is themed with, and accompanies, the same weekly Shabbat Torah reading, year on year**.

The Oleh Maftir, the person who was called up for the reading of the Torah's Maftir (concluder) section, is often the one who then sings the Haftara portion.

Whoever actually sings it, now recites the opening blessing*** for the Haftara.

This affirms the truthfulness and integrity of the Prophets.

The Haftara portion is now sung.

It concludes with four additional blessings:

1. Praising the validity and justice of Hashem's decisions;

2. Asking for mercy for Zion (Israel), our home, source of our life, and that we, her children, bring her joy;

3. Thanking Hashem for being the Shield of King David, and pledging to never let his light be extinguished;

4. Blessing Hashem for the Shabbat day, its Torah and Haftara reading, its prayers and its holiness.

---

* Haftara means, in this case; conclusion, completion, parting, taking leave of the Torah reading.

** Some Haftarot portions are linked to the time of the year, and so not related to that week's Shabbat Torah reading.

*** The same person also recites the concluding four blessings.

Track 33 **Yekum pourkan** May salvation rise up

Artscroll, Expanded: Pages 448–450, Interlinear pages 383–385.

WE PRAY TO HASHEM THAT TORAH STUDY WILL GIVE US MINDS OPEN TO ENLIGHTENMENT. PLEASE HASHEM, BLESS US AND OUR CHILDREN WITH GOOD HEALTH AND LIVES OF PURPOSE AND CONSEQUENCE.

Yeh-koum pour-kan min shmai-ya, chi-nah veh-chis-da veh-rachmey, veh-chai-yey
May salvation rise up from heaven (bringing us); grace, and loving kindness, and compassion, and a life

ariy-chey, ou-mezoh-ney reh-viy-chey, veh-siy-ata di-shmai-ya, ou-vari-youte goufa,
that is long, and an abundance of food, and heavenly assistance, and (good) health of the body,

ou-neh-hora ma-alya, zar-ah cha-ya veh-kai-yama, zar-ah di lo yifsok veh-di lo yivtol
and raised (enlightened) perception, offspring that live and endure, offspring who do not interrupt and do not cease

mi-pit-ga-mey oh-raiyta. Leh-ma-ra-nan veh-ra-ba-nan cha-vou-rata kadiysh-ata
from (their study of) the words of the Torah. (And the same also) for the masters, and rabbis, (of) the holy communities,

dibb-ar-ah deh-Israel veh-di beh-Vavel, leh-reysh-ey cha-ley, ou-leh-rey-shey galvata,
in the land of Israel and in Babylon, for the leaders of the (Torah) assemblies, and for the leaders in the exile,

ou-leh-rey-shey meh-tiy-vata, oul-dayaney di ba-va, leh-chol talmiyd-eyhon,
and for the leaders of the Yeshivot, and for the judges at the (town) gateways, for all their students,

ou-leh-chol talmiydey talmiyd-eyhon, ou-leh-chol mann deh-askiyn beh-oh-raiyta.
and for all the students of their students, and for all those who are busy with Torah (study).

Malka deh-olma yeh-varech yat-hon, ya-piysh chai-yey-hon, veh-yasgeh yomey-hon,
May the King of the world bless them, make their lives fruitful, and prolong their days,

veh-yiten ar-cha lishney-hon, veh-yit-par-koun veh-yish-tez-voun min col aka
and lengthen their years, and save and rescue them from all distress,

ou-min col marr-iyn bish-iyn. Maran di bishmai-ya yeh-heh besa-ed-hon,
and from all serious ailments. The Master who is in heaven, may He assist them,

col zman veh-idan. Veh-nomar amen.
at every time and season. And we say: Amen

Yeh-koum pour-kan min shmai-ya, chi-nah veh-chis-da veh-rachmey, veh-chai-yey
May salvation rise up from heaven (bringing us); grace, and loving kindness, and compassion, and a life

ariy-chey, ou-mezoh-ney reviy-chey, veh-siy-ata di-shmai-ya, ou-vari-youte goufa,
that is long, and an abundance of food, and heavenly assistance, and (good) health of body,

ou-neh-hora ma-alya, zar-ah cha-ya veh-kai-yama, zar-ah di lo yifsok veh-di lo yivtol
and raised (enlightened) perception, offspring that live and endure, offspring who do not interrupt and do not cease

mi-pit-ga-mey oh-raiyta. Leh-chol keh-hala ka-diysha ha-deyn, ravreh-vaya im
from (their study of) the words of the Torah. To all of this holy congregation, the elders (together) with

zeh-eh-rai-ya, tafla ou-neshai-ya, malka deh-olma yeh-varech yat-chon,
the youngsters, the infants and the women, may the King of the world bless you,

ya-piysh chai-yey-chon, veh-yasgeh yomey-chon, veh-yiten ar-cha lish-ney-chon,
make your lives fruitful, and prolong your days, and lengthen your years,

veh-tit-par-koun veh-tish-tez-voun min col aka ou-min col marr-iyn bish-iyn.
and save you and rescue you from all distress, and from all serious ailments.

Maran di bi-shmai-ya yeh-heh besa-ed-chon, col zman veh-idan. Veh-nomar amen.
The Master who is in heaven, may He assist you, at every time and season. And we say: Amen

Shabbat Shachrit (Part 1)

Track 34 Mi sh'berach He who blessed

Artscroll, Expanded: Page 450, Interlinear pages 385–386

HASHEM RECOGNISES GOOD DEEDS, GENEROSITY OF SPIRIT AND RESPECT GIVEN TO OTHERS. HASHEM BLESSES THOSE PEOPLE.

Mi sh-beh-rach avoteynou Avraham Yitzchak veh-Yaakov, hou yeh-varech
He who blessed our forefathers, Abraham, Isaac and Jacob, may He (also) bless

et col ha-ka-hal ha-kadosh ha-zeh, im col keh-hilot ha-ko-desh, hem, oun-shey-hem,
all of this holy congregation, (together) with all (other) holy congregations; them and their wives,

ouv-ney-hem, ouv-notey-hem, veh-chol ah-sher la-hem. Ou-mi sh-myach-a-diym
and their sons, and their daughters, and everything that is theirs. And to those who (unite to) establish (dedicate)

ba-tey knesi-yot li-tfi-la, ou-mi sh-ba-iym beto-cham leh-hit-palel, ou-mi sh-notniym
synagogues for prayer, and to those who come into them to pray, and to those who give

ner lama-or, veh-yai-yin leh-ki-doush ou-leh-hav-dala*, ou-fatt la-or-chiym,
a candle for illumination, and wine for the Kiddush and for the Havdala, and bread for the visitors,

outz-daka la-ani-yim, veh-chol mi sh-oskiym beh-tzor-chey tzibour beh-eh-mouna,
and charity for the poor, and to all those who are sincerely busy with the needs of the community,

ha-kadosh barouch hou yeh-sha-lem szcha-ram, veh-ya-siyr meh-hem col mach-ala,
the Holy One, Blessed is He, will pay them their reward, and will remove from them all illness,

veh-yir-pa leh-chol gou-fam, veh-yis-lach leh-chol avo-nam, veh-yish-lach bracha
and will heal their entire bodies, and will forgive all their sins, and will send blessing

veh-hatz-la-cha beh-chol ma-a-seh yeh-dey-hem, im col Israel ach-ey-hem.
and success onto every labor of their hands, (together) with all of Israel, their brothers.

Veh-nomar amen.
And we say: Amen

* Havdala is the ceremony (at the end of the Shabbat Mincha (afternoon) service) marking the end of Shabbat, and the start of the new week. The word itself means; separation.

Shabbat Shachrit (Part 1)

> # ROSH CHODESH*
> ## ON THE SHABBAT PRECEDING THE NEW MONTH ONLY.

The Four Blessings for the New Month
Only once a month

Track 35 Yehi ratzon May it be the will
Artscroll, Expanded: Page 452, Interlinear pages 387–388.

**BLESSING 1 (OF 4) FOR THE NEW MONTH.
WE PRAY TO HASHEM THAT THIS MONTH IS A TREASURE TROVE OF GOODNESS.**

Yeh-hiy ratz-on milfa-neyh-cha, Adonai Eloheynou veh-Elohey avoteynou,
May it be Your will (the will in Your presence), Hashem, our God, and the God of our forefathers,

sh-teh-cha-desh ah-ley-nou et ha-choh-desh ha-zeh leh-tova veh-liv-ra-cha.
that You renew for us this (coming) month, for goodness and (as) a blessing.

Veh-titen lanou chai-yim arou-kiym chai-yim shel shalom,
May You grant to us a life that is long, a life of peace,

chai-yim shel tova, chai-yim shel bra-cha,
a life of goodness, a life of blessing,

chai-yim shel par-nasa, chai-yim shel chi-loutz atza-mot,
a life of sustenance, a life of (good) physical health,

chai-yim sh-yesh ba-hem yir-at shamai-yim veh-yir-at chet,
a life that has within it fear (awe) of heaven, and fear of sin,

chai-yim sh-ain ba-hem bou-sha ou-chli-ma,
a life without shame and humiliation,

chai-yim shel oh-sher veh-cha-vod,
a life of wealth (plenty) and dignity,

chai-yim sh-teh-heh banou ah-havat Torah veh-yir-at shamai-yim,
a life that has within it love of Torah and fear (awe) of heaven,

chai-yim sh-yim-alou mish-alot li-benou leh-tova.
a life in which the requests of our heart are fulfilled for goodness.

Amen, selah.
Amen, forever.

* The word "Chodesh" comes from "chadash" which means new. Each month started with a new moon.

Track 36 Mi sh'asa To the One who performed

Artscroll, Expanded: Page 452, Interlinear page 388.

BLESSING 2 (OF 4) FOR THE NEW MONTH.
HASHEM, PLEASE RETURN US HOME TO OUR BELOVED LAND ISRAEL.
ALL OF ISRAEL ARE FRIENDS.

Mi sh-asa ni-siym la-ah-voteynou, veh-ga-al oh-tam meh-av-doute leh-cheh-route,
To the One who performed miracles for our forefathers, and redeemed them from slavery to freedom,

hou yig-al oh-tanou beh-karov, viy-kabetz nida-chey-nou meh-arba kanfot ha-aretz,
may He soon redeem us, and gather in (to Israel) our scattered ones from the four corners of the earth,

Cha-ver-iym col Israel* (Cha-ver-iym col Israel, Cha-ver-iym col Israel).
all of Israel are friends (all of Israel are friends, all of Israel are friends).

Veh-nomar amen.
And we say: Amen

*Whilst singing "**Chaveriym col Israel**", put your right hand on the left shoulder of the person praying next to you. We are all Israel.

Track 37 Rosh chodesh The head of the month

Artscroll, Expanded: Page 452, Interlinear page 389.

BLESSING 3 (OF 4) FOR THE NEW MONTH.

Rosh chodesh "*Nissan*"** yihi-yeh beh-yom "*rishon*"**
The head (new/first day) of the month "XXXXXX" will be on the day "XXXXXX"

ha-ba ah-leynou veh-al col Israel leh-tova.
that is coming to us and to all of Israel for goodness.

** The prayer leader will include the name of the month and the day on which it opens. Our example uses the month "Nissan" the first month of the Jewish calendar and the day "Rishon" the first day of the week (Sunday).

Track 38 Yechadshayhoo May He renew (the new month coming)

Artscroll, Expanded: Page 452, Interlinear page 389.

BLESSING 4 (OF 4) FOR THE NEW MONTH.
HASHEM, PLEASE MAKE THIS MONTH ONE OF JOY AND PEACE.

Yeh-chad-sheh-hou ha-kadosh barouch hou ah-leynou veh-al col amo beyt Israel,
May the Holy One, Blessed is He, renew it (the new month coming), on us, and on all His people, the House of Israel,

leh-chai-yim ou-leh-shalom, leh-sa-son ou-leh-sim-cha, liyi-shoua
for life and for peace, for joy and for happiness, for salvation

ou-leh-neh-cha-ma, veh-nomar Amen.
and for cheer (comfort), and we say: Amen

> **END OF THE BLESSINGS FOR THE NEW MONTH.**

Blessings for the New Month

> # MEMORIAL PRAYER
>
> OUR HEARTS CRY IN PAIN FOR OUR BROTHERS AND SISTERS OF THE HOUSE OF ISRAEL MURDERED BY DIFFERENT ENEMIES THROUGHOUT HISTORY AND STILL TODAY FOR BEING JEWISH.
>
> WE MUST ALWAYS BE ALERT TO THE EVER CHANGING THREATS AND CAPABLE OF DEFENDING OURSELVES AT ALL TIMES.

Track 39 **Av ha'rachamim shochen** Father of mercies who dwells

Artscroll, Expanded: Pages 454–456, Interlinear pages 391–393.

Av ha-rach-amiym shoh-chen meh-ro-miym, beh-rach-amav ha-atz-ou-miym
Father of mercies who dwells up on high, in His powerful compassion

hou yif-kod beh-rach-amiym, ha-chasi-diym veh-hai-sha-riym veh-ha-tmi-miym,
may He remember with compassion, the devout, and the upright (honest), and the unblemished;

keh-hilot ha-kodesh sh-masrou naf-sham al kdoushat ha-shem, ha-neh-eh-ha-viym
the holy congregations who gave up their lives for the (as a consequence of their) sanctification of the (Your) Name, they were beloved

veh-ha-neh-iy-miym beh-chai-yey-hem, ouv-motam lo nifra-dou.
and pleasant in their lifetime(s), and in their death(s) they were not (and would never be) separated (from You).

Mi-nesh-ariym kalou, ou-meh-arai-yot gav-erou, la-asot retzon koh-nam
They were lighter (more agile, swifter) than eagles, and they were stronger than lions, to perform the will of their Creator

veh-cheh-fetz tzou-ram.
and the desire of their Rock.

Yiz-keh-rem Eloheynou leh-tova, im sh-ar tzadiyk-ey oh-lam,
May our God remember them for good, (together) with (all) the other righteous (people) of the world,

veh-yin-kom leh-eyney-nou nikmat dam ava-dav ha-sha-fouch,
and may He avenge before our eyes; the vengeance for the blood of (the murdered beautiful souls) His servants that was spilt,

ka-ka-touv beh-Torat Moshe iysh ha-Elohim.
as it is written in the Torah of Moses, (the) man of God:

Har-niynou goyim amo ki dam ava-dav yi-kom, veh-na-kam ya-shiyv
O nations, sing praises with His people, for He (Hashem) will avenge the (spilt) blood of His servants, and He will exact retribution

leh-tzarav, veh-chi-perr admato amo. Veh-al yedey ava-deyh-cha
on His enemies, and (in this way) He will appease His land (and) His people (Israel). And by the hand of Your servants,

ha-nevi-iym katouv leh-eh-mor.
the prophets, it is written, saying:

Veh-ni-keti,
And (if) I (Hashem) cleanse (the wicked enemy of some sins),

DAMAM LO NI-KETI*,
I (HASHEM) WILL NOT CLEANSE (FORGIVE) THEIR (MURDEROUS) BLOODSHED (of our innocent beloved ones),

*Whilst singing "**DAMAM LO NI-KETI**", put your right hand on the left shoulder of the person praying next to you. We are all Israel.*

Shabbat Shachrit (Part 1)

va-Adonai shoh-chen beh-tZi-yon.
when Hashem dwells (again) in Zion.

Ou-veh-chit-vey ha-kodesh neh-eh-mar. Lama yomrou ha-goyim, ai-yeh Eloheyhem,
And in the holy writings, it is said: Why should the nations say "Where is their God?",

yiv-ada ba-goyim leh-ey-neynou, nik-mat dam ava-deyh-cha ha-sha-fouch. PSALM 79:10
let it be known amongst the nations, before our eyes, that the spilt blood of Your servants has been avenged.

Veh-omer: Ki doresh da-miym otam za-char, lo sha-chach tza-akat ana-viym. PSALM 9:13
And it (also) says: For the Demander of blood (justice) remembered them, He did not forget the cry of the humble ones.

Veh-omer: Ya-diyn ba-goyim maleh gvi-yot, ma-chatz rosh al
And it (also) says: He will judge the nations that are full of corpses, He will crush the (wicked) leader(s) of

eretz raba. Mi-na-chal ba-deh-rech yish-teh al ken ya-riym rosh. PSALM 110:6–7
the mighty land(s). From a river along the way He will drink (their defeat), (and) then He will (proudly) raise (His) head.

ALL PEOPLE OF GOOD FAITH

**MUST BRAVELY STAND UNITED TO MAKE SURE THAT
LOVE, FREEDOM, COMMON SENSE AND TRUTH
WIN THE BATTLE AGAINST
HATRED, COERCION, IGNORANCE AND LIES.**

Shabbat Shachrit (Part 1)

Track 40 **Ashrei yoshvei** Fortunate are those who sit

Artscroll, Expanded: Pages 456–458, Interlinear pages 393–395.

HASHEM MAKES US HAPPY.
I WILL ALWAYS PRAISE HASHEM AND SO WILL EVERYONE ELSE.

Ah-shrey yosh-vey beyt-eh-cha, od yeh-ha-leh-lou-cha selah. ^{PSALM 84:5}
Fortunate (happy) are those who sit (stay with You) in Your home (Temple), they will continually praise You forever.

Ashrey ha-am sh-ka-cha lo, ashrey ha-am sh-Adonai Elohav. ^{PSALM 144:15}
Fortunate (happy) is the nation for whom it is so, fortunate (happy) is the nation for whom Hashem is its God.

^{PSALM 145}
Teh-hila leh-David arom-im-cha Elohai ha-Meh-lech, va-avar-cha shim-cha
(King) David's psalm of praise: I will exalt You, my God, the King, and I will bless Your Name,

leh-oh-lam va-ed.
forever and ever.

Beh-chol yom avar-cheh-cha, va-aha-leh-la shim-cha leh-olam va-ed.
Every day I will bless You, and I will laud Your Name, forever and ever.

Gadol Adonai ou-meh-hou-lal meh-od veh-lig-dou-la-to ain cheh-kerr.
Great is Hashem and extolled very much, and His greatness is beyond (the reach of) investigation.

Dor leh-dor yeh-sha-bach ma-a-seyh-cha, oug-vouro-teyh-cha yagiy-dou.
Generation to (the next) generation will praise Your deeds, and they will tell of Your mighty actions.

Hadar kvod hod-eh-cha veh-divrey nif-leh-oteyh-cha asiy-cha.
The fantastic glory of Your majesty, and the subjects of Your wonders, I will tell.

Veh-eh-zouz noro-teyh-cha yo-mer-ou, oug-doulat-cha asa-preh-na.
And they will speak of Your awesome strength, and of Your greatness I will narrate.

Zeh-cher rav touv-cha yabi-you, veh-tzidkat-cha yeh-ra-neh-nou.
They will vocalize the recollection(s) of Your abundant goodness, and of Your righteousness they will sing joyfully.

Cha-noune veh-ra-choum Adonai, eh-rech apai-yim oug-dol cha-sed.
Gracious and merciful is Hashem, slow to get angry and great in loving kindness.

Tov Adonai la-col, veh-rach-amav al col ma-a-sav.
Hashem is good to everything, and His mercy is on all His works.

Yo-doucha Adonai col ma-ah-seyh-cha, va-chasi-deyh-cha yeh-var-chou-cha.
All Your works (creations) will thank You Hashem, and Your devout ones will bless You.

Kvod mal-choute-cha yo-mer-ou, oug-vourat-cha yeh-da-ber-ou.
They will speak of the honor (glory) of Your Kingdom, and they will talk of Your might.

Leh-ho-di-ya livney ha-adam gvouro-tav, ouch-vod hadar mal-chou-toh.
So as to inform mankind (the children of Adam) of His mighty deeds, and of the honor (and) splendor of His Kingdom.

Mal-choute-cha mal-choute col ola-miym, ou-memshal-teh-cha beh-chol dor va-dor.
Your Kingdom is sovereign for all eternity, and Your dominion is for every generation and generation.

Soh-mech Adonai leh-chol ha-nof-liym, veh-zo-kef leh-chol ha-kfou-fiym.
Hashem supports all the fallen, and straightens all those who are hunched.

Eyney col eh-leyh-cha yeh-sa-ber-ou, veh-ata noten la-hem et och-lam beh-ito.
All eyes (look) to You with hope, and You give (to each of) them their food (nourishment) at the (its) right time.

Po-teh-ach et yad-eh-cha, ou-masbi-yah leh-chol chai ratzon.
You open Your hand and satisfy the desire of all that is living.

Shabbat Shachrit (Part 1)

Tza-diyk Adonai beh-chol dra-chav, veh-cha-siyd beh-chol ma-a-sav.
Hashem is righteous in all of His ways, and kindly in all of His actions.

Karov Adonai leh-chol kor-av, leh-chol ah-sher yikra-ou-hou beh-eh-met.
Hashem is close to all who call upon Him, to all (those) who call Him sincerely.

Reh-tzon yeh-reh-av ya-a-seh veh-et shav-a-tam yishma veh-yo-shiy-em.
He will act on (fulfill) the wishes of those who fear Him, and He will hear their cry and He will save them.

Shomer Adonai et col oh-ha-vav, veh-et col ha-resha-iym ya-ah-shmiyd.
Hashem protects all (those) who love Him, and He will destroy all the wicked.

END OF PSALM 145

Teh-hilat Adonai yeh-daber pi, viy-varech col basar shem kodsho leh-oh-lam va-ed.
My mouth will speak praise of Hashem, and all flesh will bless His holy Name, forever and ever.

PSALM 115:18

Va-ah-nachnou neh-varech Ya meh-ata veh-ad oh-lam; halleluya.
And we will bless Yah (Hashem), from now and onwards forever, Halleluya.

**THE HOLY ARK HAS JUST BEEN OPENED.
THE PRAYER LEADER STANDS ON THE BIMAH, FACING US,
WITH THE HOLY TORAH IN THE RIGHT ARM AND SINGS.**

Track 41 Y'halleloo et shem Let them praise the Name

Artscroll, Expanded: Page 458, Interlinear page 396.

YEH-HA-LELOU ET SHEM ADONAI, KI NISGAV SHMO LEH-VADO.
Let them praise the Name of Hashem, because His Name alone is exalted.

**WE RESPOND SINGING TO THANK HASHEM FOR THE BENEFITS
WE RECEIVE FROM HIS SPLENDOR.**

Hoh-doh al eretz veh-sha-mai-yim, va-ya-rem keh-ren leh-amo,
His splendor is (everywhere) on earth and (in the) heaven(s), and He has raised the pride of His people,

teh-hila leh-chol chasiy-dav, livney Israel am kro-vo,
(and brought) praise to all His devout ones, the Children of Israel, the nation (which is) close to Him,

halleluya* (halleluya).
Halleluya (Halleluya).

*Halleluya actually means; Praise God.

Shabbat Shachrit (Part 1)

> WE SING TO ACCOMPANY THE HOLY TORAH BACK TO THE HOLY ARK.

Track 42 **Mizmor leDavid** A psalm by (King) David

Artscroll, Expanded: Page 458, Interlinear pages 397–399.

HASHEM'S VOICE REACHES EVERYWHERE.

Mizmor leh-David, ha-vou la-Adonai bney eh-liym, ha-vou la-Adonai ka-vod
A psalm by (King) David: Give (tribute) to Hashem (you) sons of deities (angels), ascribe to Hashem glory

va-oz. Ha-vou la-Adonai kvod shemo, hish-tach-avou la-Adonai
and might. Render unto Hashem (the) honor due to His Name, (and) bow down to Hashem

beh-hadrat kodesh. Kol Adonai al ha-mai-yim, El ha-kavod hirr-iym,
in (the presence of) His majestic holiness. The voice of Hashem is upon (all) the waters, the God of glory thunders,

Adonai al mai-yim ra-biym. Kol Adonai ba-ko-ach, kol Adonai beh-hadar.
Hashem's (presence) is over (all) the vast waters. The voice of Hashem appears in (full) force, the voice of Hashem appears in splendor.

Kol Adonai shoh-ver ara-ziym, vaiy-shaber Adonai et arzey ha-Levanon.
The voice of Hashem breaks the cedars, and Hashem will shatter the cedar (trees) of Lebanon.

Va-yar-kiydem kmo egel, Levanon veh-Siryon kmo ben reh-eh-miym.
And He makes them (the cedars) dance like a calf, (and the mountains of) Lebanon and Hermon (dance) like young gazelles.

Kol Adonai choh-tzev la-ha-vot esh. Kol Adonai ya-chiyl midbar,
The voice of Hashem blazes beams of fire (lightning). The voice of Hashem makes the desert shudder,

ya-chiyl Adonai midbar Ka-desh. Kol Adonai yeh-choh-lel ayalot, va-yech-eh-sof
Hashem makes the desert of Kadesh convulse. The voice of Hashem frightens the deer, and strips bare

yeh-a-rot ou-veh-heych-alo koulo omer kavod.
the forests, and (whilst) in His Temple all proclaim (His) glory.

Adonai la-maboul ya-shav, va-yeh-shev Adonai Meh-lech leh-oh-lam.
Hashem sat enthroned during the flood, and Hashem will sit enthroned, as King, forever.

Adonai oz leh-amo yiten. Adonai yeh-varech et amo ba-shalom.
Hashem will give strength to His people, Hashem will bless His nation with peace.

> **MIZMOR leDAVID is PSALM 29.**

> **THE HOLY TORAH IS NOW PUT BACK IN THE HOLY ARK AND WE SING.**

Track 43 **Oovenucho yomar**
And when it rested, he (Moses) would say

Artscroll, Expanded: Page 460, Interlinear pages 399–400.

HASHEM HAS GIVEN US HIS HOLY TORAH FOR GOOD GUIDANCE AND REMINDS US NOT TO ABANDON HER PATHWAYS FOR PLEASANTNESS.

Ou-veh-nou-cho yo-mar, shouva Adonai ri-vevot alfey* Israel.
And when it (the Holy Ark of the Covenant) was rested he (Moses) would say; Hashem come back to the multitudes of Israel.

Kouma Adonai lim-noucha-teh-cha, ata va-aron ouz-eh-cha.
Arise Hashem, to Your place of repose, You and the (holy) Ark of Your might.

Kohan-eyh-cha yil-beh-shou tzeh-dek, va-chasi-deyh-cha yeh-ra-nenou.
Your Cohanim (priests) will be clothed in righteousness, and Your devout ones will sing joyously.

Ba-a-vour David av-deh-cha, al ta-shev pney meshiy-cheh-cha.
For the sake of (King) David Your servant, do not turn away the face of (King Solomon**) Your anointed one.

Ki leh-kach tov na-ta-ti la-chem **TORATI AL TA-AH-ZOVOU**. Etz chai-yim hiy
For I have given to you good guidance, DO NOT ABANDON MY TORAH. She is a tree of life

la-ma-cha-zi-kiym bah, veh-tom-chay-ha meh-ou-shar. Dra-chay-ha dar-chey no-am,
for all those who grasp Her, and Her supporters (devotees) are happy (fortunate). Her ways are ways of pleasantness,

veh-chol netivo-tay-ha shalom. Ha-shiy-ven-ou Adonai eh-leyh-cha veh-na-shou-va,
and all Her pathways are to peace. Bring us back, Hashem, to You, and we will return,

cha-desh ya-mey-nou keh-keh-dem.
(please) renew our days (so that they are) like they (once) were before.

> **THE HOLY ARK IS NOW CLOSED.**

> **END OF SHACHRIT.**

* *Literally; "rivevot alfey" means tens of thousands (and) thousands.*

** *King Solomon eventually brought the Holy Ark (of the covenant) into the Holy Temple of Jerusalem.*

Shabbat Shachrit (Part 1)

> **THIS PRAYER SEPARATES THE SHACHRIT AND MUSSAF SECTIONS OF THE SERVICE.**

Track 44 Yitgadal, No 3 Half Kaddish

Artscroll, Expanded: Page 460, Interlinear pages 400–401.

THIRD OF 3 IN SHABBAT MORNING SERVICE.
MAY HASHEM'S NAME BE BLESSED FOREVER.

Yitgadal veh-yit-kadash shmeh raba. Beh-olma di bra kir-ou-teh
May His great Name be magnified and sanctified. In the world that He created as He wanted it,

veh-yamliych malchou-teh, beh-chai-yey-chon ou-veh-yo-mey-chon ouv-chai-yey
may His Kingship reign, in your lifetimes, and in your days, and in the lifetimes

deh-chol bet Israel, ba-agala ouvi-zman ka-riyv. Veh-imrou amen.
of all of the House of Israel, speedily and soon. And we say: Amen

Yeh-heh shmeh raba meh-vo-rach leh-oh-lam ou-leh-olmey olmai-ya.
May His great Name be blessed forever, and for all eternity.

Yit-barach veh-yishtabach veh-yitpa-ar veh-yitromam veh-yitna-seh veh-yit-hadar
Blessed, and praised, and glorified, and exalted, and upraised, and honored,

veh-yit-ah-leh veh-yit-ha-lal shmeh deh-koud-sha briych hou.
and elevated, and extolled, is the Name of the Holy One, Blessed is He.

Leh-elah min col bir-cha-ta veh-shiy-rata, toush-beh-cha-ta veh-neh-cheh-mata
Way above any blessing, and song, praise, and cheer

da-amiyran beh-olma. Veh-imrou amen.
that are vocalized in the world. And we say: Amen

Shabbat Shachrit (Part 1)

Shabbat Mussaf (additional)
The second section of the Morning Service
Part 2 of 2

> **THE START OF THE AMIDAH (STANDING) PRAYER FOR SHABBAT MUSSAF (ADDITIONAL).**
>
> **WE PRAY IT FIRST AS INDIVIDUALS AND THEN WE SING IT TOGETHER.**

Track 45 Amidah 2: Baruch ata Adonai *Blessed are You, Hashem*

Artscroll, Expanded: Page 462, Interlinear pages 402–403.

HASHEM IS THE SHIELD OF ABRAHAM, ISAAC AND JACOB, THE NATION OF ISRAEL.

(Adonai, sa-fa-tai tif-tach ou-piy yagid teh-hila-teh-cha). *Said quietly to oneself.*
Hashem, open my lips and my mouth will speak Your praise (praise You).

Barouch ata Adonai Eloheynou veh-Elohey avoteynou, Elohey Avraham,
Blessed are You, Hashem, our God, and the God of our forefathers, God of Abraham,

Elohey Yitzchak, veh-Elohey Yaakov, ha-El ha-gadol ha-gibor veh-ha-nora,
God of Isaac, and God of Jacob, the God, the Great One, the Mighty One, and the Awesome One,

El el-yon, goh-mel chasa-diym tov-iym veh-ko-neh ha-col, veh-zo-cher
the supreme God, who gives back (to us) loving kindnesses that are good, and creates everything, and remembers

chas-dey ah-vot, ou-meh-viy goh-el livney bney-hem,
the loving kindnesses of the forefathers, and brings a redeemer to the children of their children,

leh-ma-an shmo beh-ah-hava.
for the sake of His Name, with love.

Meh-lech ozer ou-mo-shiya ou-magen. Barouch ata Adonai magen Avraham.
The King who helps, saves and defends. Blessed are You, Hashem, Shield of Abraham.

Ata gibor leh-oh-lam Adonai, meh-cha-yeh metiym ata, rav leh-ho-shiya.
You are mighty forever Hashem, You resurrect the dead, You can save in abundance.

(Ma-shiyv ha-rou-ach ou-mo-riyd ha-geshem). *Only said between Simchat Torah and Pesach (the winter months).*
(You who makes the wind blow and the rain fall).

Track 46 Amidah 2: Mechalkel chaim — He nourishes the living

Artscroll, Expanded: Page 462, Interlinear page 403.

HASHEM IS FAITHFUL TO THE DEAD.
THEY REMAIN IN HIS CARE UNTIL HE RESURRECTS THEM.

Meh-chal-kel chai-yim beh-cheh-sed, meh-cha-yeh metiym beh-rach-amiym rabiym,
He nourishes the living with loving kindness, He revives the dead with abundant mercies,

soh-mech nof-liym, veh-rofeh choh-liym, ou-ma-tiyr ah-sou-riym, ou-meh-ka-yem
He supports the fallen, and He cures the ill, and He frees the captives, and He keeps

eh-mou-nato li-yesh-eney a-farr. Mi kamo-cha ba-al gvou-rot, ou-mi doh-meh lach,
His faith to those sleeping in the dust. Who is like You, Master of mighty deeds, and who is similar to You,

Meh-lech meh-miyt ou-meh-cha-yeh ou-matz-miy-ach yeh-shoua.
the King who determines death and restores life, and makes salvation sprout?

Veh-neh-eh-man ata leh-hach-yot meh-tiym.
And You are faithful to revive the dead.

Barouch ata Adonai meh-cha-yeh ha-metiym.
Blessed are You, Hashem, resurrector of the dead.

Shabbat Mussaf (Part 2)

Track 47 **Amidah 2: Naaritzcha** We will venerate You

Artscroll, Expanded: Page 464, Interlinear pages 404–405.

EVEN THE ANGELS TALK AMONGST THEMSELVES ABOUT THE HOLINESS AND GLORY OF HASHEM. HASHEM'S COMPASSION EMANATES FROM ZION, HIS BELOVED DWELLING PLACE ISRAEL.

Na-ariytz-cha veh-nak-diysh-cha keh-sod si-yach sarfey kodesh ha-makdi-shiym
We will (try to) venerate You and will (try to) sanctify You, like the secret conversation(s) of (the) holy Seraphim (angels), who sanctify

shim-cha ba-kodesh, ka-ka-touv al yad neh-viy-eh-cha, veh-kara zeh el zeh
Your Name in the Holy Sanctuary, as it is written by the hand of Your prophets; and one (angel) would call to another (angel)

veh-amar: Kadosh kadosh kadosh Adonai tzva-ot, meh-lo col ha-aretz kvodo.
and say: Holy, holy, holy, Hashem, (Lord) of the armies (of Israel), the whole earth (land) is filled with His glory.

Kvodo ma-leh oh-lam, meshar-tav sho-aliym zeh la-zeh, ai-yeh meh-kom kvodo,
His glory fills the world, His ministering (angels) ask one another, "(so) where is the abode of His glory?",

leh-ou-ma-tam barouch yomerou.
facing (one another) they proclaim, Blessed:

Barouch kvod Adonai mim-ko-mo.
Blessed is the glory of Hashem from His place.

Mim-komo hou yifen beh-rach-amiym veh-ya-chon am
From His place He will turn with compassion, and (He) will be gracious to the people

ha-myach-adiym shmo, eh-rev va-bo-ker beh-chol yom ta-miyd,
who proclaim the unity of His Name (in the) evening, and (in the) morning, every day, perpetually (day after day),

pah-amai-yim beh-ah-hava shma om-riym.
(that is) twice (each day), with love, (when) they recite the Shema:

SHMA ISRAEL ADONAI ELOHEYNOU, ADONAI EH-CHAD.
Hear O Israel, Hashem is our God, Hashem is One.

Hou Eloheynou hou ah-viy-nou hou mal-kenou, hou moshiy-enou,
He is our God, He is our Father, He is our King, He is our Savior,

veh-hou yashmiy-enou beh-rach-amav sh-niyt, leh-ey-ney col chai
and He will let us hear, in His compassion (for) a second time, before the eyes of all the living,

li-hi-yot la-chem leh-Elohim, ani Adonai Elo-hey-chem.
(His promise) "To be for You, the God, I am Hashem, your God."

Ou-veh-divrey kod-sh-cha ka-touv leh-eh-mor: Yim-loch Adonai leh-oh-lam
And in Your holy writings, it is written, saying: Hashem will reign forever;

Elohai-yich tZi-yon leh-dor va-dor, halleluya. PSALM 146:10
your God, O Zion, from generation to (the next) generation, Halleluya.

Leh-dor va-dor na-giyd godd-leh-cha
From generation to (the next) generation, we will tell of Your greatness,

ou-leh-netzach netza-chiym kdoush-at-cha nak-diysh,
and we will sanctify Your holiness forever and ever,

veh-shiv-cheh-cha Eloheynou mi-piy-nou lo ya-moush leh-oh-lam va-ed,
and praise for You, our God, from our mouth will never ever cease,

ki El Meh-lech gadol veh-kadosh ata. Barouch ata Adonai, ha-El ha-kadosh.
because God, You are a great and holy King. Blessed are You, Hashem, the holy God.

Shabbat Mussaf (Part 2)

Track 48 **Amidah 2: Tikanta Shabbat**[*] You designed Shabbat

Artscroll, Expanded: Page 466, Interlinear pages 406–409.

**HASHEM GAVE INSTRUCTIONS ON HOW TO CELEBRATE THE SHABBAT DAY.
WE PRAY TO HASHEM TO BRING US BACK UP AND PLANT US
IN OUR LAND ISRAEL WHERE WE CAN BE IN HIS PRESENCE.**

Ti-kanta Shabbat ratz-iyta korben-o-tay-ha, tzi-viyta perou-shay-ha im sidou-rey
You designed Shabbat, You wanted (to accept) Her offerings, You instructed on Her interpretations, together with the order

nesa-chay-ha, meh-angay-ha leh-oh-lam kavod yin-cha-lou, toh-amay-ha
of Her drink-offerings, (so that) those who delight in Her will inherit honor forever, (and) those who savor (taste) Her

chai-yim za-chou, veh-gam ha-oh-ha-viym dva-ray-ha gdoula bach-arou, az mi-Sinai
(will) merit (long) life, and also those who love Her words (the commandments of Shabbat) have chosen greatness, since from (Mount) Sinai

nitz-ta-vou a-lay-ha, va-tetz-ah-venou Adonai Eloheynou, leh-ha-kriyv ba
they were instructed about Her, and You commanded us, Hashem, our God, to offer up on Her,

kor-ban mousaf Shabbat ka-ra-ou-iy. Yeh-hiy ratzon mil-fa-neyh-cha,
the Shabbat Mussaf (additional) offering in the proper (deserved) way. May it be Your will (the will in Your presence),

Adonai Eloheynou veh-Elohey avoteynou,
Hashem, our God, and the God of our forefathers,

sh-ta-a-lenou beh-sim-cha leh-artz-enou, veh-tita-enou
that You bring us (back up), in happiness, to our land (Israel), and plant us

big-voul-enou, veh-sham na-aseh leh-fa-neyh-cha et kor-benot chovo-teynou,
within our border(s), and there we will perform, before You, the offerings as per our obligations (that we are duty bound to do),

tmi-diym keh-si-dram ou-mousa-fiym keh-hil-cha-tam.
the Perpetual (daily offerings) in their sequence (order), and the Mussaf (additional offerings) as per their laws.

Veh-et mousaf yom ha-Shabbat ha-zeh na-aseh veh-na-kriyv
And the Mussaf (additional offering) of this Shabbat day we will perform, and we will offer it up,

leh-fa-neyh-cha beh-ah-hava, keh-mitzvat retzon-eh-cha, kmoh sh-ka-tavta ah-leynou
before You (in your presence), with love, as it is commanded as You wanted, as You wrote (down) for us

beh-Torah-teh-cha, al yeh-dey Moshe av-deh-cha, mi-pi kvo-deh-cha ka-ah-mour.
in Your Torah, by the hand of Moses Your servant, from Your glorious mouth, as it is said:

---

[*] *This prayer is not part of the service on the Shabbat preceding the New Month.*

Shabbat Mussaf (Part 2)

Track 49 Amidah 2: Ooveyom ha'Shabbat, & Yismechu

And on the day of Shabbat, & They will be happy

Artscroll, Expanded: Page 468, Interlinear pages 410–412.

THOSE WHO KEEP THE SHABBAT UNDERSTAND THE HAPPINESS OF BEING A JEW.

Ou-veh-yom ha-Shabbat shney kva-siym bney sha-na tmi-iy-mim,
And on the day of Shabbat (the offering is to be), two unblemished (male) lambs in their first year,

ou-shney es-roniym solet min-cha blou-la ba-sheh-men veh-nisko.
and a two-tenth (measure) of an ephah of fine flour (for the) meal offering, mixed with (olive) oil and its drink-offering (tribute wine).

Olat Shabbat beh-Shabbato, al olat ha-ta-miyd veh-niska.*
The Shabbat Elevation offering (only) on its (specific) Shabbat, (and is) in addition to the Perpetual (daily) Elevation offering, and its drink-offering (tribute wine).

Yis-meh-chou beh-malchoute-cha shom-rey Shabbat veh-kor-ey oh-neg,
They will be happy in (accepting) Your Kingship, those who keep the Shabbat and call it a delight,

am meh-kad-shey shvi-iy, kou-lam yisbeh-ou veh-yit-an-gou mi-tou-veh-cha,
the people (Children of Israel) who sanctify the seventh (day), will all be satisfied and delighted from Your goodness,

ouva-shvi-iy ra-atz-iyta bo veh-ki-dash-toh, chem-dat ya-miym oto ka-rata,
and You favored (coveted) the seventh (day) and sanctified it, You called it the most treasured of days,

zeh-cher leh-ma-aseh beh-reh-shiyt.
a reminder of the (Your) Act of Creation (of the world).

On the Shabbat preceding the New Month, additional prayers are now added before Yismechou.

Track 50 **Amidah 2: Elohanu*** Our God

Artscroll, Expanded: Page 468, Interlinear pages 412–413.

HASHEM, PLEASE MAKE US DESERVING AND CAPABLE OF KEEPING YOUR HOLY SHABBAT.

Elo-heynou veh-Elohey avo-teynou, reh-tzeh bim-noucha-tenou.
Our God, and the God of our forefathers, (please) find favor in our rest.

Kad-sh-nou beh-mitzvo-teyh-cha, veh-ten chel-kenou beh-Torah-teh-cha. Sab-enou
Make us holy with Your commandments and (please) give us our place (heritage/birthright) in Your Torah. Satisfy us

mi-tou-veh-cha, veh-samm-chen-ou bi-yeshoua-teh-cha, veh-ta-herr li-benou
with Your goodness, and make us happy in Your salvation, and purify our heart(s),

leh-ov-deh-cha beh-eh-met. Veh-han-chiy-lenou Adonai Eloheynou
to serve You with sincerity. And bequeath to us, Hashem, our God,

beh-ah-hava ou-veh-ratzon Shabbat kod-sh-cha, veh-ya-nou-chou bo Israel
with love and with favor, Your holy Shabbat, and Israel will rest on it,

meh-kad-shey shmeh-cha. Barouch ata Adonai, meh-ka-desh ha-Shabbat.
the sanctifiers of Your Name. Blessed are You, Hashem, who sanctifies the Shabbat.

* There is a different Elohanu prayer on the Shabbat preceding the New Month.

Shabbat Mussaf (Part 2)

Track 51 **Amidah 2: Retze, & Ve'techezeyna**
Find favor, & May we witness

Artscroll, Expanded: Page 470, Interlinear page 414.

THANK YOU HASHEM FOR RETURNING TO ZION.
WE BLESS YOU HASHEM FOR RESTORING YOUR DIVINE PRESENCE IN ISRAEL.

Reh-tzeh Adonai Eloheynou beh-am-cha Israel ouvi-tfila-tam, veh-ha-shev
Hashem, our God, find favor in Your people Israel and in their prayer, and return

et ha-avoda li-dviyr beyt-eh-cha
the worship to the (rebuilt) sanctuary of Your Temple (in Jerusalem),

veh-ishey Israel ou-teh-fi-la-tam beh-ah-hava teh-kabel
and accept the fire-offerings and prayer of Israel with love

beh-ratzon, ou-teh-hiy leh-ratzon ta-miyd avodat Israel am-eh-cha.
and favor, and may the worship of Israel, Your people, always be appealing (to You).

Veh-teh-cheh-zeyh-na ey-ney-nou beh-shouv-cha leh-tZi-yon beh-rach-amiym.
And may our eyes witness Your return to Zion in compassion.

Barouch ata Adonai, ha-mach-ziyr shchiyn-ah-toh leh-tZi-yon.
Blessed are You, Hashem, who restores His divine presence to Zion.

Shabbat Mussaf (Part 2)

Track 52 **Amidah 2: Modim** Thanks

Artscroll, Expanded: Pages 470–472, Interlinear pages 414–417.

**WE HAVE LIFE THANKS TO HASHEM'S CONTINUOUS WONDERS AND MIRACLES.
WE THANK HASHEM FOR VALUING US AND CARING FOR US EVERY MINUTE OF EVERY DAY.**

Moh-diym ah-nachnou lach, sh-ata hou Adonai Eloheynou veh-Elohey avoteynou
We thank You, that it is You who is Hashem, our God, and the God of our forefathers,

leh-oh-lam va-ed. Tzour chai-yeynou, magen yish-enou, ata hou leh-dor va-dor.
for all eternity. Rock of our lives, Shield of our salvation, it is You from generation to (the next) generation.

Noh-deh leh-cha oun-sa-perr teh-hila-teh-cha al chai-yeynou hamm-sou-riym
We will thank You and we will verbalize Your praise, for our lives that are committed

beh-yad-eh-cha, veh-al nish-moh-teynou hap-koudot lach, veh-al ni-seyh-cha
into Your hand, and for our souls that are entrusted to You, and for Your miracles

sh-beh-chol yom ima-nou, veh-al nif-leh-oteyh-cha veh-tovo-teyh-cha sh-beh-chol et,
that are with us every day, and for Your wonders and Your favors that are (with us) at all time(s),

eh-rev va-bo-ker veh-tzo-hoh-ra-yim. Ha-tov ki lo ka-lou rach-ah-meyh-cha,
evening, and morning and afternoon. (You are) the Good One because (as) Your mercy never depletes,

veh-hamm-ra-chem ki lo tamou chasa-deyh-cha, meh-oh-lam ki-viy-nou lach.
and the Merciful One, because (as) Your loving kindnesses never end, our hope has always been to You.

Veh-al koulam yit-barach veh-yit-romam shim-cha mal-kenou tamiyd
And for all of these (things) may Your Name, our King, be continuously blessed and exalted,

leh-oh-lam va-ed.
forever and ever.

Veh-chol ha-chai-yim yoh-dou-cha selah, vi-yeh-ha-lelou et shim-cha beh-eh-met.
And all that is alive will give gratitude to You forever, and will praise Your Name with sincerity.

Ha-El yeh-shoua-tenou veh-ezra-tenou selah.
The God of our salvation and of our succor, forever.

Barouch ata Adonai ha-tov shim-cha ou-leh-cha na-eh leh-ho-dot.
Blessed are You, Hashem, the Good One is Your Name, and to You it is fitting to give thanks.

Shabbat Mussaf (Part 2)

Track 53 Amidah 2: Elohanu v'Elohai avotanu barchanu, & Sim Shalom
Our God and God of our forefathers bless us, & Establish peace

Artscroll, Expanded: Page 472, Interlinear pages 417–418.

PLEASE HASHEM LIGHT UP YOUR FACE TOWARDS US, BE GRACIOUS TO US AND ESTABLISH PEACE FOR US.

Eloheynou veh-Elohey avo-teynou bar-chen-ou ba-bra-cha ha-meh-shou-leh-shet
Our God, and the God of our forefathers, bless us with the triple (three verse) blessing

ba-Torah, hak-touva al yedey Moshe av-deh-cha, ha-ah-moura mi-pi Aharon
in the Torah, written by the hand of Moses Your servant, (and) as spoken from the mouth of Aaron

ou-va-nav, Koha-niym am kedosh-eh-cha ka-amour.
and his sons, the Priests, Your holy people, as it is said:

Yeh-va-rech-eh-cha Adonai veh-yish-meh-reh-cha.
May Hashem bless you and protect you.

Ya-er Adonai pa-nav eh-leyh-cha viy-chou-neh-ka.
May Hashem light up His face towards you, and be gracious to you.

Yi-sah Adonai pa-nav eh-leyh-cha, veh-ya-sem leh-cha shalom.
May Hashem turn His face towards you, and establish peace for you.

WE THANK HASHEM FOR HIS HOLY TORAH WHICH TEACHES US TO LOVE BEING KIND AND FOR MAKING US A NATION THAT YEARNS FOR PEACE.

Siym shalom toh-va ouv-ra-cha, chen va-cheh-sed veh-rach-amiym ah-leynou
Establish peace, goodness, and blessing, grace, and loving kindness and mercies on us,

veh-al col Israel ah-meh-cha. Bar-chen-ou aviy-nou, kou-lanou keh-eh-chad beh-orr
and on all Israel, Your people. Bless us, our Father, all of us as one (single person), with the light

pan-eyh-cha, ki beh-orr pan-eyh-cha na-ta-ta la-nou, Adonai Eloheynou,
of Your face, because through the light of Your face, You gave us, Hashem, our God,

Torat chai-yim veh-ah-ha-vat cheh-sed outz-daka, ouv-ra-cha, veh-ra-cha-miym,
the Torah of Life, and (through Her) a love for loving kindness, and charity, and blessing, and compassion,

veh-chai-yim, veh-shalom. Veh-tov beh-ey-neyh-cha leh-va-rech et am-cha Israel
and life, and peace. And may it be (it is) good in Your eyes to bless, Your people, Israel,

beh-chol et ou-veh-chol sha-ah bi-shlom-eh-cha.
at every time, and at every hour, with Your peace.

Barouch ata Adonai, ha-meh-va-rech et amo Israel ba-shalom
Blessed are You, Hashem, who blesses His people, Israel, with peace

(et amo Israel ba-shalom).
(His people, Israel, with peace).

END OF THE (REPETITION OF THE) MUSSAF AMIDAH.

Track 54 **Yitgadal, No 2 Full Kaddish**

Artscroll, Expanded: Page 474, Interlinear pages 420–422.

SECOND OF 2 IN SHABBAT MORNING SERVICE.
HASHEM PLEASE GRANT ISRAEL LIFE AND PEACE.

Yit-gadal veh-yit-kadash shmeh raba. Beh-olma di bra kir-ou-teh
May His great Name be magnified and sanctified. In the world that He created as He wanted it,

veh-yamliych malchou-teh, beh-chai-yey-chon ou-veh-yo-mey-chon ouv-chai-yey
may His Kingship reign, in your lifetimes, and in your days, and in the lifetimes

deh-chol bet Israel, ba-agala ou-vizman ka-riyv. Veh-imrou amen.
of all of the House of Israel, speedily and soon. And we say: Amen.

Yeh-heh shmeh raba meh-vo-rach leh-oh-lam ou-leh-olmey olmai-ya.
May His great Name be blessed forever, and for all eternity.

Yit-barach veh-yishtabach veh-yitpa-ar veh-yitromam veh-yitna-seh veh-yit-hadar
Blessed, and praised, and glorified, and exalted, and upraised, and honored,

veh-yit-ah-leh veh-yit-ha-lal shmeh deh-koudsha briych hou.
and elevated, and extolled, is the Name of the Holy One, Blessed is He.

Leh-elah min col bir-cha-ta veh-shiy-rata toush-beh-cha-ta veh-neh-cheh-mata
Way above any blessing, and song, praise, and cheer

da-amiyran beh-olma. Veh-imrou amen.
that are vocalized in the world, and we say: Amen.

Titkabel tzlot-hon ouva-oute-hon deh-chol bet Israel ka-dam avou-hon
(Please) accept the prayers and (humble) appeals, of the whole House of Israel, (placed) before their Father

di bishmai-ya. Veh-imrou amen.
in heaven. And we say: Amen.

Yeh-heh shlama raba min shmai-ya, veh-chai-yim ah-leynou veh-al col Israel.
May there be abundant peace from heaven, and life for us and for all Israel.

Veh-imrou amen.
And we say: Amen.

Oseh shalom bimro-mav, hou ya-aseh shalom ah-leynou, veh-al col Israel.
He who makes peace in His heights, may He make peace for us and for all Israel,

Veh-imrou amen.
And we say: Amen.

Shabbat Mussaf (Part 2)

Track 55 **Kaveh** Hope (in Hashem)

Artscroll, Expanded: Page 476, Interlinear page 422.

WE PLACE OUR HOPE IN HASHEM BUT HE ALSO EXPECTS FROM US TO BE STRONG.

Ka-veh el Adonai, cha-zak veh-ya-ah-metz li-beh-cha,
(Place your) hope in Hashem, be strong and He will give courage to your heart,
_{PSALM 27:14}
veh-ka-veh el Adonai. Ain kadosh ka-Adonai, ki ain bil-teh-cha,
and (keep your) hope in Hashem. Nothing is holy like Hashem, for there is nothing without You,

veh-ain tzour keh-Elo-heynou. Ki mi Elo-ha mibal-adey Adonai
and there is no Rock like our God. For who is God other than Hashem,

oumiy tzour zou-la-ti Elo-heynou. _{PSALM 18:32}
and who is a Rock other than our God ?

Track 56 **Ain ke'Elohanu** Nothing is like our God

Artscroll, Expanded: Page 476, Interlinear pages 422–423.

HASHEM IS UNIQUE.

Ain keh-Elo-heynou, ain ka-Ado-neynou, ain keh-mal-kenou, ain keh-moshiy-enou.
Nothing is like our God, nothing is like our Master, nothing is like our King, nothing is like our Savior.

Mi keh-Elo-heynou, mi ka-Ado-neynou, mi keh-mal-kenou, mi keh-moshiy-enou.
Who is like our God, who is like our Master, who is like our King, who is like our Savior ?

Nodeh leh-Elo-heynou, nodeh la-Ado-neynou, nodeh leh-mal-kenou,
We will thank our God, we will thank our Master, we will thank our King,

nodeh leh-moshiy-enou. Barouch Elo-heynou, barouch Ado-neynou,
we will thank our Savior. Blessed is our God, blessed is our Master,

barouch mal-kenou, barouch moshiy-enou. Ata hou Elo-heynou,
blessed is our King, blessed is our Savior. You are our God,

ata hou Ado-neynou, ata hou mal-kenou, ata hou moshiy-enou.
You are our Master, You are our King, You are our Savior.

Ata hou sh-hik-tiyrou avo-teynou leh-fa-neyh-cha et ktoret ha-sa-miym.
It was for You, that our forefathers burned, in front of You, the incense of spices.

Shabbat Mussaf (Part 2)

Track 57 P'toum ha'ketoret The mix of incenses

Artscroll, Expanded: Page 476, Interlinear pages 423–424.

THE INSTRUCTIONS FOR PREPARING THE INCENSES FOR THE OFFERINGS TO HASHEM IN THE HOLY TEMPLE OF JERUSALEM.

Pi-toum hak-toret: Ha-tzari veh-ha-tzipoh-ren ha-chel-bena veh-hal-vona, mish-kal
The mix of incenses: Stacte (sweet oil), and the onycha, the galbanum and frankincense (each) weighing

shiv-iym shiv-iym ma-neh; Mor, ouk-tziya, shi-bolet nerd, veh-charr-com, mish-kal
seventy (exactly) seventy maneh; (And) myrrh, and cassia, spikenard, and saffron (each) weighing

shi-sha asar shi-sha asar ma-neh. Ha-kosht shneym asar, veh-ki-loufa shlosha,
sixteen (exactly) sixteen maneh; (And) the costus (weighing) twelve (maneh), and aromatic bark (weighing) three (maneh),

veh-kinamon tisha. Bo-riyt kar-shiyna tisha ka-biyn,
and cinnamon (weighing) nine (maneh). (And) nine kav's of Lye from Carshina,

yain kafri-siyn seh-iyn teh-la-ta veh-kabiyn teh-la-ta, veh-im ain lo yain kafri-siyn,
three seah's and three kav's of Cyprus wine, and if he has no Cyprus wine,

mev-iy cha-mar chi-var-yan atiyk, meh-lach sdo-miyt rova ha-kav.
he is to bring (use) aged pale wine. (And) a quarter of a kav of salt from Sodom.

Ma-aleh ah-shan col sh-hou.
(And) a tiny amount from a smoke (producing) herb.

Ra-bi Natan ha-Bavli oh-mer: af kipat ha-yarden col sh-hou.
Rabbi Natan of Babylon says: a tiny amount of Jordan amber as well.

Veh-im natan ba dvash, psa-la. Veh-im chis-ar ah-chat mi-col
And (that) if he put honey in it (the mixture), he invalidated it. And (that) if he missed out (even) one from all

sa-ma-nay-ha, chai-yav miy-ta.
her (the mixture's) spices, he is liable for the ultimate punishment (from heaven).

Track 58 Raban Shimon Rabbi Shimon

Artscroll, Expanded: Pages 476–478, Interlinear pages 424–425.

RABBI SHIMON BEN GAMLIEL WAS PRESIDENT OF THE SANHEDRIN (JEWISH SUPREME COURT) AND KILLED BY THE ROMANS FOR SUPPORTING THE JEWISH REVOLT. GAMLIEL MEANS "MY REWARD IS GOD".

Raban Shimon ben Gamli-el oh-mer: Ha-tzari eyno eh-la sraf ha-notef
Rabbi Shimon son of Gamliel declares: The stacte is nothing other than the sap that drips

meh-atzey hak-taff. Bo-riyt kar-shiyna sh-sha-fiyn ba et ha-tzipoh-ren keh-dey
from (the tapping of the wood) of the balsam trees. Lye from Carshina is used to bleach the onycha so that

sh-teh-heh na-ah. Yain kafri-siyn sh-sho-riyn bo et ha-tzipoh-ren keh-dey
it will be beautiful; Cyprus wine is used to soak the onycha so that

sh-teh-heh aza; va-ha-loh mey rag-lai-yim ya-fiyn la,
it will have a powerful aroma, even though urine is good for it (this purpose);

eh-la sh-ain mach-ni-siyn mey rag-lai-yim ba-azara
but they are not to (do not) bring urine into the Temple

mi-pney ha-ka-vod.
out of respect.

Shabbat Mussaf (Part 2)

Track 59 **Ha'shir sh'haLeviyim** The song that the Levites

Artscroll, Expanded: Page 478, Interlinear pages 425–426.

WE SING THE SAME SONG OF PRAISE TO HASHEM THAT THE LEVITES WHO ASSISTED THE KOHANIM USED TO SING IN THE HOLY TEMPLE OF JERUSALEM.

Ha-shiyr sh-ha-Levi-yim ha-you om-riym beh-veyt ha-mik-dash.
The song that the Levites would recite (each day of the week) in the Holy Temple.

Ba-yom ha-rishon* ha-you om-riym;
On the Sunday they would recite;

La-Adonai ha-aretz oum-lo-ah teh-vel veh-yosh-vey ba. PSALM 24:1
To Hashem belongs the earth, and its fullness, (and) the world and those who live in it.

Ba-sheni* ha-you om-riym;
On the Monday they would recite;

Gadol Adonai ou-meh-houlal meh-od, beh-iyr Eloheynou har kodsho. PSALM 48:2
Hashem is great and hugely lauded, in the city of our God, the Mountain of His Holiness (Jerusalem).

Ba-shliyshi* ha-you om-riym;
On the Tuesday they would recite;

Elohim nitz-av ba-adat El, beh-keh-rev Elohim yish-pot. PSALM 82:1
God stands in the divine assembly, amongst deities, (and) He (alone) will make judgement.

Barr-vi-iy* ha-you om-riym;
On the Wednesday they would recite;

El neh-kamot Adonai El neh-ka-mot ho-fiy-ah. PSALM 94:1
O God of retribution, Hashem, O God of retribution appear.

Ba-cha-miy-shi* ha-you om-riym;
On the Thursday they would recite;

Har-niy-nou leh-Elohim ouz-enou hari-you leh-Elohey Yaakov. PSALM 81:2
Sing joyously to the God (the source) of our strength, applaud the God of Jacob.

Ba-shishi* ha-you om-riym;
On the Friday they would recite;

Adonai ma-lach geh-oute la-vesh, la-vesh Adonai oz hit-azar
Hashem reigned clothed in grandeur, Hashem has clothed and girded Himself with might,

af tikon teh-vel bal timot. PSALM 93:1
(and) has established the world so it would not collapse.

Ba-shabbat ha-you om-riym;
On the Shabbat they would recite;

Miz-mor shiyr leh-yom ha-shabbat. Mizmor shiyr leh-atiyd la-vo, leh-yom
A psalm, a song (in honor of) for the Shabbat day. A psalm, a song for the future to come – for the day

sh-koulo Shabbat ou-meh-nou-cha leh-chai-yey ha-oh-la-miym.
that is the absolute Shabbat and respite, for a life that is everlasting (in this world and the world to come).

Literally; "On the first day", "On the second day" etc.

Shabbat Mussaf (Part 2)

Track 60 **Tana d'vai Eliyahu, & Amar Rabbi Elazar**
It was taught in Elijah's synagogue, & Rabbi Elazar said

Artscroll, Expanded: Page 478 Interlinear pages 426–428.

THE TORAH IS THE LIFE SOURCE OF JUDAISM, THE JEWISH NATION AND ISRAEL. IT IS FROM THE TORAH THAT WE HAVE GROWN, IT IS THE TORAH THAT TAUGHT US TO LOVE TO LEARN, DISCOVER AND CREATE.

Ta-na dvey Eli-ya-hou col ha-shoh-neh hala-chot beh-chol yom,
It was taught in the Bet Midrash of Elijah (the prophet), that everyone who studies the laws (of the Torah) every day,

mouv-tach loh sh-hou ben oh-lam ha-ba, sh-neh-eh-mar: Haliy-chot oh-lam loh,
is ensured participation in the world to come, as it is said: The ways of the world are His,

al tik-rey ha-liy-chot, eh-la ha-la-chot.
(but) do not call them "ways", but instead (call them) laws (Hashem's laws).

Amar Ra-bi El-azar amar Ra-bi Cha-niy-na; tal-midey cha-cha-miym marbi-iym
Rabbi Elazar said that Rabbi Chanina stated: wise students (Torah scholars) increase

shalom ba-oh-lam sh-neh-eh-mar. Veh-chol ba-nai-yich limou-dey Adonai,
peace in the world, as it is said: And all your children (of Israel) will be students (in the Torah) of Hashem,

veh-rav shlom ba-nai-yich, al tik-rey ba-nai-yich
and your children (will have) abundant peace, (but) do not call them "your children",

eh-la bo-nai-yich.
but instead (call them) "your builders" (because they are Torah scholars).

<u>Shalom rav leh-oh-ha-vey Torah-teh-cha,</u>
There is abundant peace for those who love Your Torah,

<u>veh-ain lamo mich-shol.</u> Yeh-hiy shalom beh-chey-lech, shalva beh-armeno-tai-yich. PSALM 119:165
and there is no obstacle for them. May there be peace within your wall(s), and tranquility in your palaces (Jerusalem).

<u>Leh-ma-an ach-ai veh-reh-ai, adabra na shalom bach.</u>
For the sake of my brothers and my friends, I will talk, therefore, (in my prayer) of your peace (Jerusalem).

<u>Leh-ma-an beyt Adonai Eloheynou, avaksha tov lach.</u> PSALM 122:7–9
For the sake of the House of Hashem, our God, I will request good for you (Jerusalem).

<u>Adonai oz leh-amo yi-ten, Adonai yeh-varech et amo ba-shalom.</u> PSALM 29:11
Hashem will give strength to His people, Hashem will bless His people with peace.

**MOURNERS ONLY NOW RECITE A KADDISH PRAYER
CALLED THE RABBIS' KADDISH.**

Shabbat Mussaf (Part 2)

Track 61 **Aleynu leshabayach, & Al ken nekave**
It is our duty to praise, & That is why we hope

Artscroll, Expanded: Pages 480–482, Interlinear pages 430–432.

WE PRAY THAT HASHEM PERFECTS THE WORLD SO THAT EVEN THE WICKED WILL KNOW HIM AND REPENT FOR THE SAKE OF GOODNESS.
WE ARE GRATEFUL THAT WE ARE JEWS WHO BELIEVE IN HASHEM.

A-leynou leh-sha-beh-ach la-Ah-don ha-col, la-tet gdoula leh-yotzer beh-reh-shiyt,
It is our duty to praise the Master of everything, to attribute greatness to the Molder of the beginning (of the world),

sh-lo asa-nou keh-goy-yey ha-ara-tzot, veh-lo sa-manou keh-mish-peh-chot
that He did not make us like the nations of the (other) lands, and did not place us (deem us) like the (other) families

ha-ada-ma. Sh-lo samm chel-kenou ka-hem, veh-gora-lenou keh-chol ha-moh-nam.
of the earth. That He did not make our portion like theirs, nor our fate like all their masses.

Va-anachnou ko-riym ou-mishtach-aviym ou-mo-diym, lif-ney Meh-lech mal-chey
And we bend (our knees), and bow down and give thanks, before the King, (the) King of

hamm-la-chiym ha-kadosh barouch hou. Sh-hou noteh shamai-yim veh-yosed aretz,
the kings, the Holy One, Blessed is He. That it is He, who stretches out the heavens and establishes the earth,

ou-moshav yeh-karo ba-shamai-yim mi-ma-al, ou-shchiy-nat ou-zo
and the abode of His glory is in the heaven(s) above, and the divine presence of His might,

beh-govhey mro-miym.
is in the elevated heights.

Hou Eloheynou, ain od. Eh-met mal-kenou, eh-fes zou-lato, ka-ka-touv
He is our God, there is no other. Our King is the truth, there is zero other than Him, as it is written

beh-Torah-toh; veh-ya-da-ta ha-yom va-ha-sheh-vota el leh-va-veh-cha, ki Adonai
in His Torah; and you will know today and you will take it to your heart, that Hashem

hou ha-Elohim ba-sha-mai-yim mi-ma-al veh-al ha-aretz mi-ta-chat ain od.
is the God in the heavens above, and on the earth below, (and that) there is nothing else.

Al ken neh-ka-veh leh-cha Adonai Eloheynou lir-ot meh-heh-ra beh-tif-eh-ret
That is why we hope to You, Hashem, our God, to rapidly see the splendor

ou-zeh-cha, leh-ha-a-viyr gilou-liym min ha-aretz,
of Your might; eliminating idols from the earth,

veh-ha-eli-liym karot yika-reh-toun,
and destroying (all) the (false) deities completely,

leh-ta-ken oh-lam beh-mal-choute sha-dai veh-chol bney ba-sar yikreh-ou
(thereby) perfecting the world through the Kingship of the Almighty, and all flesh (people) will call

bi-shmeh-cha leh-haf-not eh-leyh-cha col rish-ey aretz. Ya-kiyrou veh-yeh-dou
Your Name, (and at that time even) all the wicked of the earth will (also) turn to You. They will recognise and will know,

col yosh-vey teh-vel, ki leh-cha tich-ra col beh-rech, tish-ava col la-shon.
all the dwellers of the world, that to You every knee will bend, (and) every tongue will pledge (allegiance).

Leh-fa-neyh-cha Adonai Eloheynou yich-reh-ou veh-yi-po-lou,
Before You, Hashem, our God, they will bend (their knees) and will fall down,

veh-lich-vod shim-cha yeh-kar yit-enou.
and to the honor of Your Name they will pay homage.

Viy-kablou kou-lam et ol malchou-teh-cha, veh-tim-loch a-ley-hem meh-heh-ra
And all will accept the servitude to Your Kingdom, and You will, very soon (speedily) rule over them,

leh-oh-lam va-ed. Ki ha-mal-choute shel-cha hiy ou-leh-olmey ad tim-loch beh-chavod,
forever and ever. For the sovereignty is Yours, and You will reign, with glory, forever and ever,

ka-ka-touv beh-Torah-teh-cha Adonai yim-loch leh-oh-lam va-ed.
as it is written in Your Torah: Hashem will reign forever and ever.

Veh-neh-eh-mar veh-ha-ya Adonai leh-Meh-lech al col ha-aretz, ba-yom ha-hou
And it is said; Hashem will be the King upon all the earth, (and) on this day,

yihi-yeh Adonai eh-chad ou-shmo eh-chad.
Hashem will be One, and His Name will be One.

Track 62 **Al tira** Do not fear

Artscroll, Expanded: Page 482, Interlinear page 432.

HASHEM DESPISES EVIL. THE WICKED WILL NEVER TRIUMPH. HASHEM IS WITH US.

Al tiyra mi-pach-ad pit-om ou-mi-shoh-at resha-iym ki tavo
Do not fear from sudden terror, and nor from destruction by the wicked when it approaches,

oute-tzou etza veh-tou-farr
(they) make a (wicked) plan and it will be nullified,

dabrou davar veh-lo ya-koum,
(they) speak a (wicked) word (declaration) and it will not stand up (happen),

ki imanou El (ki imanou El).
because God is with us (because God is with us).

Veh-ad zikna ani hou, veh-ad sey-va ani esbol,
And (even) until (your) old age I (Hashem) am (still) the same, and (even) until (your) white hairs I will carry you,

ani a-siyti va-ani eh-sa (ani a-siyti va-ani eh-sa, ani a-siyti va-ani eh-sa)
I (Hashem) made (you) and I will support (you), (I made (you) and I will support (you), I made (you) and I will support (you)),

va-ani esbol va-amalet.
and I (Hashem) will carry and rescue (you).

MOURNERS ONLY NOW RECITE THE MOURNER'S KADDISH.

Shabbat Mussaf (Part 2)

> # SHIR HA-KAVOD
> ### THE HOLY ARK IS OPENED FOR THE SONG OF GLORY.

Track 63 **Anim zmirot** I will compose pleasant psalms
Artscroll, Expanded: Pages 484–486, Interlinear pages 434–438.

MY HEART AND SOUL ARE CONNECTED TO HASHEM AND MAKE ME ALWAYS WANT TO SING SONGS OF LOVE TO HIM.
HASHEM HONORS THE HUMBLE NOT THE ARROGANT.
IT IS OUR DUTY TO RISE TO THE CHALLENGE TO MAKE HASHEM PROUD OF US.

> ### PRAYER LEADER CHANTS, THEN CONGREGATION RESPONDS.

Ah-niym zmiy-rot veh-shiy-riym eh-eh-rog ki eh-leyh-cha naf-shiy ta-arog.
I will compose pleasant psalms and weave songs (of love for You) because my soul yearns for You.

Nafshiy cham-da beh-tzel yad-eh-cha la-da-at col raz sod-eh-cha.
My soul desires (to shelter in) the shade of Your hand, (and) to know all the mystery of Your secret(s).

Mi-dey da-briy bich-vo-deh-cha hoh-meh li-bi el do-deyh-cha.
Whenever I speak of Your glory, my heart pines for Your love.

Al ken ad-aber beh-cha nich-badot veh-shim-cha acha-bed beh-shiyr-ey yeh-diydot.
So I will speak of You and Your glories, and I will honor Your Name with love songs.

Asapra kvod-cha veh-lo reh-iy-tiy-cha adam-cha achan-cha veh-lo yeh-da-tiy-cha.
I will tell of Your glory even though I have not seen You, I will imagine and describe You even though I have not known You.

Beh-yad neh-viy-eyh-cha beh-sod ava-deyh-cha di-miyta hadar kvod hodeh-cha.
By the hand of Your prophets and the counsel of Your servants, You made us imagine the magnificence of the glory of Your majesty.

Gdou-lat-cha ou-gvoura-teh-cha kinou leh-toh-kef peh-oula-teh-cha.
Your greatness and Your might, they described based on the validity of Your (awesome) actions.

Di-mou ot-cha veh-lo keh-fi yesh-cha vai-yeh-sha-vou-cha leh-fi ma-aseyh-cha.
They imagined You but not as You actually are, and valued You based on Your deeds.

Himm-shiy-lou-cha beh-rov chez-yo-not hin-cha eh-chad beh-chol dim-yo-not.
They compared You to many visions, but You are One in all imaginations.

Va-yech-eh-zou beh-cha zikna ou-va-cha-route ou-seh-ar rosh-cha beh-seyva
They saw in You (both) age (maturity) and youth, and the hair on Your head as white

veh-sha-cha-route.
and as black.

Zikna beh-yom diyn ou-va-cha-route beh-yom krav keh-iysh mil-cha-mot
Aged (mature) on the day of judgement, and youthful on the day of battle, like a warrior

ya-dav lo rav.
whose hands fight for him (skillfully).

Shabbat Mussaf (Part 2)

Cha-vash kova yesh-oua beh-rosho ho-shiya lo yeh-miyno ou-zroa kodsho.
He wore the hat of salvation on His head, it was salvation for Him, His right hand and His holy arm.

Ta-leh-ley oh-rot rosho nim-la kvoutzo-tav resi-sey lai-la.
His head is filled by the dew drops of light, His locks (of hair) by the night rains.

Yitpa-er bi ki cha-fetz bi veh-hou yihi-yeh li la-a-teh-ret tzvi.
He will glory in (be proud of) me because He desires in me, and He will be for me a crown of beauty.

Ketem tahor paz dmoute ro-sho veh-chak al metz-ach kvod shem kod-sho.
Fine pure gold is the image of His head, and inscribed on His forehead is the glory of His holy Name.

Leh-chen oul-cha-vod tzvi tif-ah-ra ou-ma-to lo itra ata-ra.
For His grace and for His glory, His beauty (and) His splendor, His nation decorated Him with a crown.

Mach-leh-fot ro-sho kiv-yimey beh-chou-rot kvoutzo-tav tal-taliym shcho-rot.
The locks of hair on His head are as (of) the days of youth, His locks are black curls.

Neh-veh ha-tzedek tzvi tif-arto ya-a-leh na al rosh sim-cha-toh.
The abode of righteousness (Jerusalem), its beauty and its splendor, may it rise above His uppermost joy.

Sgoula-toh teh-hiy beh-yado ah-teh-ret ou-tzniyf meh-lou-cha tzvi tif-eh-ret.
His treasured people should be like a crown in His hand, and like a royal tiara of beauty (and) splendor.

Amou-siym nesa-am ah-teh-ret in-dam meh-ah-sher ya-krou beh-eynav kib-dam.
He carried them from birth, He wore them like a crown, (and) because they were precious in His eyes, He honored them.

Peh-eh-ro a-lai ou-feh-eh-riy a-lav veh-karov eh-lai beh-koriy eh-lav.
His splendor is upon me and my splendor (when I am wearing Tefillin) is upon Him, and He is close to me when I call to Him.

Tzach veh-ah-dom lil-vousho ah-adom poura beh-darko beh-vo-oh meh-eh-dom.
He is pure (with compassion) and red (with anger), His garment is red like when treading the winepress, when He returns (after executing judgement) from Edom.

Keh-sher tfi-liyn herr-ah leh-anav tmou-nat Adonai leh-neh-ged ey-nav.
He showed the tefillin knot to the humble one (Moses), a depiction of Hashem (was) in front of his eyes (revealed to him).

Ro-tzeh beh-amo ana-viym yeh-fa-er yoshev teh-hilot bam leh-hitpa-er.
He desires for His people, He will glorify the humble, seated on (their) praises, in them He glories.

Rosh dvar-cha eh-met ko-reh meh-rosh dor va-dor am doresh-cha drosh.
Your first word (from the Torah) is truth, it calls from the beginning to all generations; to the people who seek You, (please) respond.

Shiyt ha-mon shiy-rai na a-leycha veh-rinatiy tikrav eh-leycha.
Please place my abundance of songs before You, and my joyous singing will come close to You.

Teh-hilati teh-hi leh-rosh-cha ah-teret ou-tfi-lati ticon keh-toret.
May my praise be a crown for Your head, and may my prayer be accepted like (the Temple) incense.

Tiykar shiy-rat rash beh-ey-neyh-cha ka-shiyr youshar al korban-eyh-cha.
May the song of the poor man be precious in Your eyes, like the song that is sung (by the Levites) on offerings to You.

Birkati ta-aleh leh-rosh mash-biyr meh-choh-lel ou-mo-liyd tza-diyk ka-biyr.
May my blessing rise up (and reach) to the head (crown) of the Sustainer, Creator, and Giver of Life, (the) Righteous, Mighty One.

Ou-veh-virkati tna-ana li rosh veh-ota kach leh-cha kiv-sa-miym rosh.
And (when) I bless You (please) nod Your head to me, and (please) accept it for yourself as (you would accept) the finest spices.

Yeh-eh-rav na siy-chi a-leyh-cha ki nafshi ta-arog eh-leyh-cha.
Please may my speech be pleasant to You, because my soul yearns for You.

THE HOLY ARK IS NOW CLOSED. ALL OF US SING TOGETHER AGAIN.

Shabbat Mussaf (Part 2)

Leh-cha Adonai ha-gdoula veh-ha-gvoura veh-ha-tif-eh-ret veh-ha-netzach
To You, Hashem, is the greatness, and the might, and the splendor, and the victory,

veh-ha-hod ki col ba-sha-mai-yim ou-va-aretz.
and the majesty, because everything in the heaven(s) and on the earth (is Yours).

Leh-cha Adonai ha-mamm-la-cha veh-ha-mitna-seh leh-chol leh-rosh.
Hashem, Your's is the Kingship and the supremacy over every leader.

Mi yeh-ma-lel gvourot Adonai yash-miy-ya col teh-hi-lato. PSALM 106:2
Who is (even remotely) capable of expressing the heroics of Hashem, of making all of His praise(s) heard ?

Track 64 **Adon olam** Master of the world

Artscroll, Expanded: Page 12, Interlinear page 129.

**THE CREATOR OF THE WORLD IS FOREVER.
HASHEM IS ALWAYS WITH ME AND I WILL NOT FEAR.**

Ah-don oh-lam ah-sher ma-lach beh-teh-rem col yeh-tziyr niv-ra.
Master of the world who reigned (even) before any form (creation) was created (by Him).

Leh-et na-asa beh-cheff-tzo col, ah-zai Meh-lech shmo nikra.
At the (very) moment everything was made by His will, then (immediately) His Name was proclaimed as King.

Veh-ach-rey kich-lot ha-col leh-va-do yim-loch nora.
And after everything has ended (this world is no more), He alone will (still) reign in awesomeness.

Veh-hou ha-ya veh-hou hoh-veh veh-hou yihi-yeh beh-tif-ah-ra.
And it is He who was, and He who is, and He who will be, (as always) in splendor.

Veh-hou eh-chad veh-ain sh-ni leh-hamm-shiyl lo leh-hach-biyra.
And He is unique, and there is no second one to compare to Him, as an equal (to associate with Him).

Bli reh-shiyt bli tach-liyt, veh-lo ha-oz veh-ha-misra.
(He is) without a beginning (and) without an end, and to Him is (belongs) the might and the supremacy.

Veh-hou eh-li veh-chai goh-ah-li veh-tzour chev-li beh-et tza-ra.
And He is my God, and my living Redeemer, and my Rock (against) misfortune in time of trouble.

Veh-hou nisi ou-ma-nos li, meh-nat kosi beh-yom eh-kra.
And He is my battle flag (miracle) and (also) my refuge, (He is) my cup's portion (my fate) on the day I call (Him).

Beh-yado af-kiyd rou-chi beh-et iy-shan veh-ah-iy-ra veh-im rou-chi gviy-ati
Into His hand I deposit (entrust) my spirit when I go to sleep, and (again) when I wake up; and (together) with my spirit, my body as well,

Adonai li veh-lo iy-ra.
Hashem is with me and I will not fear.

Ah-don oh-lam ah-sher ma-lach beh-teh-rem col yeh-tziyr ni-vra.
Master of the world who reigned (even) before any form (creation) was created (by Him).

Leh-et na-asa beh-cheff-tzo col ah-zai Meh-lech shmo nikra.
At the (very) moment everything was made by His will, then (immediately) His Name was proclaimed as King.

Friends, now we have kiddush together
Shabbat Shalom

The beating heart of our community

A healthy diaspora Jewish community is judged by its synagogue(s), not the bricks and mortar, but as places where we want to go because we feel that sense of "it's my place too".

When we are there we behave better, it brings out the best in all of us. We are respectful to one another, we feel connection and friendship. It is a place of escape from outside pressures and negative influences, we walk in and we immediately de-stress.

The synagogue represents Jewish civilisation, from here emanates our moral principles, laws and purpose; it is our heart, it is our home, all the rest sits on this foundation.

Let's sing together, all of us, as one, and fill our synagogues every Shabbat.

The most commonly used words for a Synagogue* are:

HEBREW

Bet Knesset   House of Gathering/Assembly/Bringing together, in

Bet Tfila   House of Prayer

Bet Midrash   House of Study (literally; demanding an explanation)

YIDDISH

Shul   comes from the German "Shule" for school (via the Latin word Schola).

Shtiebel   means a little house/room, and comes from the Yiddish "Shtub" and German "Stube" for room.

*Synagogue is actually the Greek translation of the Hebrew, Bet Knesset.

Richard Collis

Mum & Dad,
Edie & Gerald Collis.
I have been blessed.

Yossi Yoffe

Special thanks

Natan Collis For singing with me through every stage of the project, you were part of its evolution and fulfillment.

Talia Collis For your belief in me and the kiruv (outreach) goal of sharing our prayers with everyone.

Ariel Felber of Jerusalem. For your help with the understanding and articulation of the Hebrew.

Rabbi Menachem Salaman of Stamford Hill, London.
For your kindness, your insights and for your advice.

Rabbi Steve (Yitzhak) Ginsberg of Beirav Carlebach Synagogue, Safed, Israel. For wanting to help and for your generosity of spirit. Your inspiration made it possible for me to realise the dream.

Yossi Yoffe of London. For putting your heart and soul into making beautiful music for this mitzvah project.

Michele Quastel For your encouragement and support.

Credits

Yossi Yoffe Musical director, arranger and backing vocals.
www.vocaltrack.co.uk

wesingwestaytogether.com